Originally published in 2021 by Amazon Publishing

All rights reserved. No part of this publication may be reproduced, stored in a retrieval system, or transmitted, in any form or by any means, electronic, mechanical, photocopying, recording, or otherwise without prior written permission from the publisher.

Amazon Publishing
Seattle, WA

ISBN-13: 979-8-5333-5138-6
ISBN-10: 8-5333-5138-6

Printed and bound in the United States by CreateSpace, An Amazon.com Company

TABLE OF CONTENTS

INTRODUCTION

PART I – MULTI-MILLION DOLLAR COMPANIES

Letter 1: Relocation to North Carolina - (Amtrak Train) – December 1993
- Stranded on track in Manassas, Virginia
- Visit to Martin Luther King Memorial 20 Years Later

Letter 2: Oil Change - (Jiffy Lube) – 1996 to 2000

Letter 3: Too Big to Fail – (Carnival Cruise Line) - September 12, 2009
- Carnival Cruise Line Mishaps
- Carnival Stock Prices
- Carnival Demise (2020)

Letter 4: Kentucky Derby - (Hampton Inn) – May 2019
- Restoration of Points

PART II – HOME IMPROVEMENT AND UPGRADES

Letter 5: Sump Pump Installation - (B-Dry System) – May 2005
- Reinstallation - June 6, 2005
- Installation 3 – July 8, 2005

Letter 6: Patio Enclosure and Deck Installation - (Honey Doer) – September 16, 2006
- Death of Partner
- Hospitalization of Owner

Letter 7: Roof Replacement - (Priority One) – August 12, 2011
- Work Authorization
- Contract – July 22, 2011
- Scheduling Concerns
- Request for Refund
- Certificate of Satisfaction

Letter 8: Sprinkler System Installation - (Water Saver Irrigation, Inc.) – August 6, 2014

Letter 9: Damaged Pipes - (Well Doctor) - March 2019
- Depth of Trench
- Leaky Tank
- Busted pipe
- Life-Time Warranty

PART III- REAL ESTATE

Letter 10: Payoff of Principal - (Wells Fargo Amortizations) – 2010 to 2011
Letter 11: Retroactive Tax Assessment – (Mecklenburg County Tax Assessment 2011-2014) – May 24, 2016
Letter 12: Giving the Gift of a Home - (My Home) – December 2019
Letter 13: Home Appraisal Challenge – (Samaritan's House Inc.) - January 6, 2020

PART IV – LEGAL RESOLUTION

Letter 14: Cease and Desist Order - (Straight Arrow Construction) – September 19, 2007
- North Carolina Licensing Board Claim
- Response from North Carolina Licensing Board
- Design Developers Complaint
- Response from Licensing Board – Injunction against Design Developer

Letter 15: Landscaping – (Intrinity Landscaping, LLC) – June 21, 2014
- Signed Proposal
- Memo to the File 7/19/2014
- Requests to Replace Dead Sod
- Memo to the File 9/5/2014
- Dispute of Charges to Bank of America
- Metro Greenscape – Second Opinion
- Engagement Letter 5/27/2015
- Department of Justice Correspondences – 6/1/2015, 6/22/2015, 7/10/2015
- Counter Suit – Court date 11/20/2015
- Judgement
- Mutual Dismissal with Prejudice

PART V – TRANSPORTATION

Letter 16: Moving from Philly - (Stevens Relocation) – September 12, 2014
- Where are They Now?

Letter 17: Potholes Blow-out on Thanksgiving Day - (NC Department of Transportation) – November 22, 2018
- New Tires and Rims Pictures
- Discount Tire Receipt
- NC DOT Citizen Incident Statement - 1/19/2019
- Pictures of Damage to Vehicle Tires and Rims
- Claim Denied – 3/9/2019
- Response to Department of Justice Attorney General
- Measuring the NC DOT Performance and Accountability

PART VI – INSURANCE COMPANIES

Letter 18: Increase in Allstate Premiums - (CitiMortgage Homeowners' Insurance) – November 18, 2016

Letter 19: Insurance Cancellations (Farm Bureau, Zurick, BCBS, State Farm, IBC, Allstate, Liberty Mutual) – 1990 to 2020
- Farm Bureau
- Zurick Medallion
- BCBSNC
- State Farm
- IBC – Independent Blue Cross
- Allstate
- Liberty Mutual

Letter 20: Hurricane Florence – (Liberty Mutual Insurance Company) – September 2018
- Due Diligence – 9/24/2018
- Claim Denied – 9/25/2018
- Update on Due Diligence – 10/8/2018

- November 9, 2018 Correspondences
- Letter to Liberty Mutual President and NC Insurance Commissioner
- Response from President Service Team
- Response from NC Department of Insurance
- Consent Rate
- Where are They Today (9/16/2020)

PART VII – MISCELLANEOUS

Letter 21: Bunion Surgery - (Charlotte Foot Clinic) – December 7, 2007

Letter 22: Parking Lot Scam - (Habitat Restore) – November 1, 2014

Letter 23: Mentors and Protégé – (Warren Buffett) - October 2016
- Letter to Warren Buffett
- Response from Buffett Assistance – 11/3/2016
- Follow-up Letter to Warren Buffett – 4/18/2017

Letter 24: Raccoons Above Ceiling – (The Tradition Apartments) – June 15, 2020

Getting off the Grid

INTRODUCTION

Isaiah 54:17 - No weapon that is formed against thee shall prosper; and every tongue that shall rise against thee in judgment thou shalt condemn. This is the heritage of the servants of the Lord, and their righteousness is of me, saith the Lord. (KJV)

AMERICA!! AMERICA!! God shed his grace on thee and crown thy good with brotherhood from sea to shining sea.

Around the world, America is viewed as the land of prosperity. You can be or do anything that you put your mind to. This is somewhat true. Because of this belief, individuals, companies, and the government offer products and services to the everyday consumer. The consumer then pays for those products and services and expects a certain level of honesty, quality, and safety.

There are laws that govern and protect consumers as they relate to products and services. For example, the Consumer Protection Act that was implemented in 1986, gives easy and fast compensation to **consumer** grievances. It safeguards and encourages consumers to speak against insufficiency and flaws in goods and services. The consumer also has certain rights and responsibilities. I am highlighting those rights and responsibilities below for information purposes.

The Rights of the Consumer

- **Right to Safety** - Before buying, a consumer can insist on the quality and guarantee of the goods.
- **Right to Choose** - Consumer should have the right to choose from a variety of goods and at a competitive price.
- **Right to be informed** - The buyers should be informed with all the necessary details of the product, make her/him act wise, and change the buying decision.
- **Right to Consumer Education** - Consumer should be aware of his/her rights and avoid exploitation. Ignorance can cost them more.
- **Right to be heard** - This means the consumer will get due attention to express their grievances at a suitable forum.
- **Right to seek compensation** - This defines that the consumer has the right to seek redress against unfair and inhumane practices or exploitation of the consumer.

The Responsibilities of the Consumer

- **Responsibility to be aware** – A consumer has to be mindful of the safety and quality of products and services before purchasing.
- **Responsibility to think independently** – Consumer should be well concerned about what they want and need and therefore make independent choices.
- **Responsibility to speak out** - Buyer should be fearless to speak out their grievances and tell traders what they exactly want.
- **Responsibility to complain** - It is the consumer's responsibility to express and file a complaint about their dissatisfaction with goods or services in a sincere and fair manner.
- **Responsibility to be an Ethical Consumer** - They should be fair and not engage themselves with any deceptive practice.

This book is a collection of letters that I have written over the years dealing with products and services that have been provided by individuals, businesses, corporations, and the government that have been flawed.

My main purpose is to highlight the ordeals I had to go through to resolve conflicts, challenges, disputes and or to obtain justice. Even though, America is the land of plenty, flowing with milk and honey, there is still a lot to be desired.

Please travel with me as I share my stories in the following letters.

PART I
MULTI-MILLION DOLLAR COMPANIES

LETTER 1: Relocation to North Carolina
(Amtrak Train) - December 1993

In December 1993, I decided to accept a position with VF Corporation and relocate to Greensboro, North Carolina. The movers had come and packed up the house a few days before me and the kids were to drive to Greensboro, NC.

The night before we were supposed to drive to Greensboro, there was a snowstorm in Ohio. According to the news, the roads were treacherous, and I could not even get out of my neighborhood.

We could not stay in the house because I had the power cut-off as of the date we had planned to leave, and there was no heat. I left my 1987 Volvo in the garage and planned to fly back a few days later to get it once the roads had cleared up.

So, we ended up getting train tickets to go to Greensboro, North Carolina. We called a taxi to take us to the train station. Once we got out of the neighborhood and onto the interstate, the roads were drivable.

Stranded on track in Manassas, Virginia

Nevertheless, the train trip was unforgettable. Somewhere out in the middle of Manassas, Virginia, the train stopped on the tracks. We were stranded there with no heat or food. Amtrak had to fly in engineers to repair the train after several hours of being on the track. There was no backup train to come get us.

Once the train was repaired, we then had to wait at another train station for hours until a train came to take us on to Greensboro, North Carolina.

I wrote a letter to the President of Amtrak at that time expressing my concerns with the train trip. Amtrak sent me a voucher for $200 or more to be used on a future train trip. I ended up giving that voucher to my brother, and he used it on a round trip from Alabama to New York. I vowed that I would never ride an Amtrak train again.

After I flew back to my house in Ohio to get my car a few days later, I noticed there was a leak in the ceiling in the bathroom near the sunroom which was across from the pool. I call "Mat", one of my neighbors I had rented a house from when I initially moved to Ohio to come over and see if he could fix the leak. He was able to fix the leak, and I was on my way back to North Carolina in a few hours.

Visit to Martin Luther King Memorial 20 Years Later

During the weekend of April 27, 2012, approximately 20 years later, I did take a trip from Charlotte to Washington, DC on Amtrak to visit the Martin Luther King Memorial located in West Potomac Park next to the National Mall with some friends of mine. The train ride was enjoyable during the trip to and from Washington, DC.

LETTER 2: Oil Change
(Jiffy Lube) - 1996 to 2001

While working at Sara Lee Hosiery in Winston-Salem, NC; I took my 1981 Mazda GLC to get my oil changed on University Blvd one day. When I got my car back, I noticed that it was leaking oil. I went back to the shop to let them know that my oil was not leaking before I came in to have it changed. They indicated that they did not have anything to do with the oil leaking.

I wrote a letter to Jiffy Lube's Corporate Office explaining my experience at the store in Winston-Salem on University Blvd. The district manager came to Winston-Salem, picked my car up at my job location, took it to the Jiffy Lube store and corrected the problem. He even credited my account for what I had paid for the oil change. This is an example of great customer service and the value of the company's image and brand.

LETTER 3: Too Big to Fail
(Carnival Cruise Line) - September 12, 2009

During the month of September 2009, my sister contacted me concerning a friend of hers that had paid to go on a Carnival Cruise and would not be able to go. The cruise was supposed to go the Cayman Islands, Jamaica and one other location. She asked me if I was interested in buying her reservation and going in her place. I said yes.

I made reservations to fly into Orlando Florida to get on the cruise ship that was sailing on September 12, 2009.

Once we got on the ship and was in the line to go through the security checkpoint, we were given a letter of a change in our itinerary. Carnival Cruise Line indicated that due to a problem with the "Rotors" of the ship, they were unable to travel to a faraway distance. So, they decided to cruise to Key West Florida and the Bahamas instead. We could see Key West Florida while we were still docked in Port Canaveral in Orlando Florida, and the Bahamas was only a skip and a hop away. I was livid!!!

I was unable to get off the ship and get my luggage. If I had any idea of this change prior to me getting on the ship, I would have gone back to the airport and got a ticket to return to Charlotte the same day I arrived in Orlando. During the entire cruise, I did absolutely nothing. I lounged on the upper deck for the duration of the cruise because I had no interest in the Bahamas or Key West.

After returning to Charlotte and a few weeks later, my daughter indicated that some of her co-workers had gone on the Carnival Cruise ship the following week and were told the same thing about the ship "Rotors", and they only went to Key West, Florida and the Bahamas.

This revealed to me that Carnival Cruise Line was taking advantage of individuals and purposely not upholding their part of the contract to cruise to the islands we had paid for.

As compensation for the change of destination, Carnival indicated they would be giving passengers 50% discount off their next cruise. I had no plans to ever cruise Carnival again.

I wrote to Carnival Cruise Line requesting a full refund. I received a letter back indicating that they have a right to change the cruise destination for whatever reasons they see fit.

I then wrote a letter to the President of Carnival Cruise Line at that time summarizing the concerns noted above. I also mentioned that Carnival Cruise Line may appear to be almighty today, but it will be just a matter of time before you fall.

Shown below are excerpts from some of the mishaps that Carnival Cruise Line has experienced subsequently to me writing a letter to the President of Carnival indicating their demise.

Carnival Cruise Line Mishaps:

September 30, 2009: Carnival Legend crashes into Royal Caribbean Enchantment of the Seas.

On September 30, 2009, as Enchantment of the Seas was berthed at Cozumel, high winds pushed the **cruise ship Carnival** Legend against the side resulting in **damage**.

November 9, 2010: Carnival Splendor Cruise Ship Stranded in the Pacific.

SAN DIEGO -- A cruise ship stranded offshore with 4,500 passengers and crew must be towed slowly into a Mexican port and will not arrive until at least Wednesday night, the Coast Guard said today. The Carnival Splendor was 200 miles south of San Diego when an engine room fire cut its power early Monday, according to a statement from Miami-based Carnival Cruise Lines. The 3,299 passengers and 1,167 crew members were not hurt, and the fire was put out, but the 952-foot ship had no air conditioning, hot water, or telephone service. Auxiliary power allowed toilets and cold running water to be restored Monday night.

January 13, 2012: Carnival's Costa Allegra Concordia in Italy – 32 Dead.

On 13 January 2012, the **Italian cruise ship Costa Concordia** ran aground and overturned after striking an underwater rock off Isola del Giglio, Tuscany, resulting in **32 deaths**. The eight-year-old **Costa Cruises vessel** was on the first leg of a **cruise** around the Mediterranean Sea when she deviated from her planned route at the Isola del Giglio, sailed closer to the island, and struck a rock formation on the sea floor. This luxury cruise ship operated by Carnival's Costa Cruises brand, was grounded on rocks off the Tuscan island of Giglio in Italy.

March 31, 2012: Carnival cruise ship briefly seized in Texas.

U.S. marshals briefly seized a cruise ship in coastal Texas on Saturday under a judge's order in a $10 million lawsuit filed on behalf of a woman who died in the Italian cruise ship disaster. The Carnival Triumph was seized for several hours at its port in Galveston, where it was scheduled to leave with 2,700 passengers. Both sides said they reached a confidential deal late Saturday afternoon that released the ship for its five-day cruise to Mexico.

The lawsuit, filed on behalf of the estate of Siglinde Stumpf, claims that Carnival shared responsibility for Stumpf's death for not preparing and maintaining proper safety programs for all vessels under its control, including the ill-fated Costa Concordia.

February 11, 2013: Carnival Triumph Cruise Ship stranded in Gulf of Mexico.

Passengers on a Carnival Triumph cruise ship drifting in the Gulf of Mexico aren't getting the vacation they expected -- sleeping on its decks, making do with a few working toilets, and doing what they can to get food -- all due to a weekend engine fire left the vessel dead in the water. The Carnival Triumph was about 150 miles off the coast of Mexico's Yucatan Peninsula, heading back Sunday morning to Galveston, Texas -- where it had departed Thursday on a four-day trip -- when a fire broke out in an engine room, according to Carnival Cruise Lines. This fire left the ship -- and its 3,143 passengers and 1,086 crew members -- adrift without propulsion, the cruise line said, halting its trip back to port.

March 14, 2013: Carnival Cruise ship stranded in the Caribbean's.

The Carnival Dream ship stranded in St. Martens because the emergency generator that operates their propulsion failed. There were 4300 passengers on board.

May 5, 2018: Carnival Cruise Line apologizes after a water line breaks in the ships.

A **broken water line** left the **Carnival Dream cruise ship** flooded throughout hallways and 50 staterooms last Thursday as crew members rushed to restore rooms and resettle passengers within a matter of hours.

November 3, 2018: Passengers panicked after Carnival Cruise ship tips.

PORT CANAVERAL, Fla. — *A technical malfunction caused a Carnival Cruise to tip on its side, evoking panic in many passengers. According to People, the Carnival Sunshine ship tipped on its side Sunday night after a switchboard malfunctioned. One passenger indicated that, "It kept leaning. Plates and silverware started sliding off the tables. Then the tables themselves started to slide. Glasses and plates started to fall and shatter. At this point, it was pure chaos. Screams. Cries. Panic."*

December 20, 2019: Two Carnival Cruise ships crashes into each other Cozumel Mexico.
A Carnival cruise ship smashed into another cruise ship — and nearly clipped a second vessel — while docking at a port in Mexico Friday morning, according to videos from the scene. The massive Carnival Glory was sailing into a dock in Cozumel at 8:50 a.m. when it struck the Carnival Legend, which was already anchored nearby, the cruise ship company told Fox61.com. At least six people suffered minor injuries on Glory as groups of guests were being evacuated from third and fourth floor dining rooms after the crash, according to the outlet. The Legend is reportedly based in Tampa, Florida, and the Glory is based in New Orleans.

Carnival Stock Prices

The following table was obtained from the internet on July 15, 2020, of Carnival Annual Stock Price. As you can see that in 2009 the average price of the stock was $27.0781 with a year close of $31.69. As of today, July 15, 2020, the average price of stock is $24.5448 and the year close is $15.04.

Carnival Historical Annual Stock Price Data

Year	Average Stock Price	Year Open	Year High	Year Low	Year Close	Annual % Change
2020	24.5448	51.3100	51.9000	7.9700	15.0400	-70.41%
2019	49.5631	49.8500	58.8500	40.1300	50.8300	3.10%
2018	62.3047	66.7500	71.9400	46.2100	49.3000	-25.72%
2017	62.8625	52.1400	69.4800	52.1400	66.3700	27.49%
2016	48.4264	54.2000	54.6800	41.9200	52.0600	-4.44%
2015	48.7652	45.6100	55.1400	42.6500	54.4800	20.19%
2014	39.2830	39.8100	45.9500	33.8800	45.3300	12.85%
2013	35.5141	37.5000	40.1700	31.6000	40.1700	9.25%
2012	34.0656	32.9600	39.3200	29.4800	36.7700	12.65%
2011	36.9060	46.8100	47.8500	29.4200	32.6400	-29.21%
2010	37.2492	32.0600	46.5900	30.1400	46.1100	45.50%
2009	27.0781	25.5500	33.9500	16.9800	31.6900	30.30%
2008	35.1157	43.6600	44.7800	15.0200	24.3200	-45.34%
2007	47.3818	50.9500	52.3900	42.2300	44.4900	-9.30%
2006	46.1640	54.5700	55.9000	36.4100	49.0500	-8.27%
2005	52.4663	57.3100	58.4500	46.5500	53.4700	-7.22%
2004	46.4798	39.8200	58.7400	39.8200	57.6300	45.05%
2003	30.6256	25.6300	39.7300	20.7500	39.7300	59.24%
2002	27.7481	27.6500	34.5800	22.3000	24.9500	-11.15%
2001	28.0094	20.3100	33.8100	18.0500	28.0800	-8.86%
2000	26.2152	46.8800	50.5600	18.6300	30.8100	-35.56%
1999	45.4963	45.4400	53.5000	39.1300	47.8100	-0.40%
1998	33.2224	27.1900	48.0000	21.6900	48.0000	73.35%
1997	20.9760	15.8750	27.6900	15.8150	27.6900	67.82%
1996	14.3094	12.4400	16.5000	11.6875	16.5000	35.36%
1995	11.6268	10.1250	13.5000	10.1250	12.1900	14.73%
1994	11.4083	11.6875	13.0000	9.7200	10.6250	-10.30%
1993	9.8736	8.2200	12.1875	7.8125	11.8450	44.67%
1992	7.3101	6.4375	8.4375	6.2800	8.1875	24.76%
1991	5.4675	3.5300	7.1875	3.0950	6.5625	85.91%
1990	4.5871	5.0000	6.1875	2.7500	3.5300	-28.97%

Demise (2020)

July 15, 2020: Carnival stock is trading at $17.47. If you look at Carnival Cruise Line stock prices over the last 30 years, it is lower than what it was 20 years ago.

August 18, 2020: Ransomware Attack Hits Carnival Cruise Corporation - headline.

"Talk about kicking someone, or some organization, when it's down. The Carnival Corporation, which has canceled cruises for months now as a result of COVID-19, says one of its cruise brands was hit with a ransomware cyberattack. Carnival owns Carnival Cruise Line, Princess Cruises, Holland America Line, Seabourn, P&O Cruises (Australia), Costa Cruises, AIDA Cruises, P&O Cruises (UK), and Cunard. The cruise line did not specify which of its cruise brands was impacted. Right now, everything we know comes from the company's special filing with the U.S. Securities and Exchange Commission, notifying the SEC of the data breach.

- Hackers encrypted some files
- Hackers exfiltrated (removed) some data
- Remediation is underway

Here is Carnival Corporation's ransomware and cyber incident statement, in full:

> *On August 15, 2020, Carnival Corporation and Carnival PLC (together, the "Company," "we," "us," or "our") detected a ransomware attack that accessed and encrypted a portion of one brand's information technology systems. The unauthorized access also included the download of certain of our data files.*

Promptly upon its detection of the security event, the Company launched an investigation and notified law enforcement, and engaged legal counsel and other incident response professionals.

While the investigation of the incident is ongoing, the Company has implemented a series of containment and remediation measures to address this situation and reinforce the security of its information technology systems. The Company is working with industry leading cybersecurity firms to immediately respond to the threat, defend the Company's information technology systems, and conduct remediation.

Based on its preliminary assessment and on the information currently known (in particular, that the incident occurred in a portion of a brand's information technology systems), the Company does not believe the incident will have a material impact on its business, operations, or financial results.

Nonetheless, we expect that the security event included unauthorized access to personal data of guests and employees, which may result in potential claims from guests, employees, shareholders, or regulatory agencies. Although we believe that no other information technology systems of the other Company's brands have been impacted by this incident based upon our investigation to date, there can be no assurance that other information technology systems of the other Company's brands will not be adversely affected."

These are examples of the demise of a corporation that thought it was so big and mighty in 2009.

LETTER 4: Kentucky Derby
(Hampton Inn) - May 2019

On 5/1/2019, a friend and I went to the Kentucky Derby at Churchill Downs in Louisville, Kentucky. We stayed at the Hampton Inn in Elizabethtown, Kentucky.

Approximately a year prior to this time in 2018, I had made reservations through Hilton Honors systems to stay at this Hampton Inn. I used most of my Hilton Honors points as well as paid approximately $300 to secure the room for 5 nights. The average price of the room was approximately $500 due to this being Kentucky Derby week.

When I checked out of the hotel on 5/5/2019, I was billed $254.44. This amount had been automatically charged to my credit card. I indicated to the Desk Clerk that I had paid for my stay in full and in advance using Hilton points and the remainder in cash/credit card. Of course, the local hotel did not have this information on file. Nevertheless, my question was how this amount of $254.44 was determined. This question was not answered.

The hotel manager was not on site for me to resolve the issue before I traveled back to North Carolina.

I later received an email asking me to complete a survey of my stay at the Hampton Inn. I completed the following survey with a rating of "**1 – Extremely Dissatisfied**".

After returning to Charlotte, North Carolina I immediately contacted Hilton's corporate office with my concern. See file number referenced in document below:

Email Response 1:

Hilton - Feedback regarding your recent stay (File number : 25784956)

Dear ABBIE THORNTON,

Thank you for taking the time to reach out to share your concerns. It was my pleasure to assist you with the concerns you have expressed with your recent stay. We take your feedback very seriously and will do everything possible to resolve your concerns in a satisfactory manner as quickly as possible.

Please allow us 72 business hours to resolve this matter for you. If you have any additional questions or concerns please feel free to contact us at (888) 240-6152 or via email at Guest.Correspondence@HRCC-Hilton.com. We will be more than happy to assist you.

We know you have a choice in where you stay when you travel and we do appreciate you choosing Hilton.

Sincerely,

Monet
Guest Assistance Specialist
Hilton Guest Assistance

Email response 2:

Restore of Points

As a result of me expressing my dissatisfaction regarding this situation, over 100,000 of my points were restored to my account. See below:

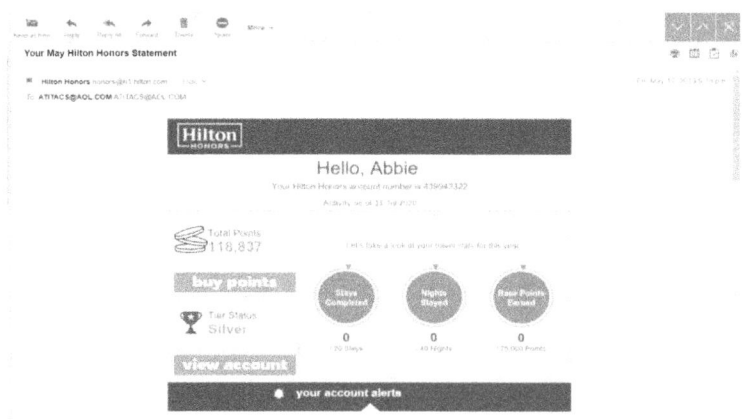

As a result of Hilton responding and acting timely to my concern, I decided to accept the restoring of my point as sufficient compensation instead of disputing the charge with my credit card company. This is an example of good customer service.

PART II

HOME IMPROVEMENT

LETTER 5: Sump Pump Installation
(B-Dry Systems) - May 2005

During May 2005, I contracted with B-Dry System to install a sump pump in my basement. The owner of the company came to my home to explain the process of installing the sump pump. We discussed the related warranties etc., and then scheduled an installation date.

As a part of the installation, a French drain had to be dug inside and across the front perimeter of my home, and then along the right side. They had to break the concrete flooring in my basement to dig the drain. I was physically at my home while the work was being done and watched the installers during the entire process.

I mentioned to the foreman of the job at that time that I did not think the drain was deep enough when they were about to put the rocks in the drain. He replied that he had been doing this for so many years and knew what he was doing. I said OK, but I still do not think it is deep enough. He was not happy with me. So, the crew completed the installation by putting the rocks over the pipes, covered the drain with cement and went their way after a few days of working in my home.

Approximately two weeks later we had a hard rain. I came home from work one day and saw the water standing in my basement garage from the newly installed drain overflowing.

I contacted the owner of the company and indicated that I had expressed my concerns of the drain not being deep enough initially to the foreman.

Re-installation

On June 6, 2005, the installation crew had to come back to my house to dig up the concrete again and make the French drain deeper. Over the next few weeks, I watched the area around the French drain to see if there were any issues related to water seepage or overflow.

On July 7, 2005, I contacted the owner via the letter below regarding additional issues with the second installed drain.

2135 Light Brigade Drive
Matthews, North Carolina 28105
July 7, 2005

Stephen LaDue, Owner
3191 Amity Hill Road
Statesville, NC 28677

Hello Mr. LaDue:

This memo is just a follow-up to our conversations concerning the area in the garage floor that was opened to flush water through the pipes after the re-installation on June 6, 2005 of pipes in the basement area.

I have been watching the area for the last several weeks. The first heavy rain that I received was on June 27 and June 28. At that time, I noticed two (2) wet spots along the garage wall close to the garage door.

On today, July 7th there was a very noticeable wet spot in the utility room in the basement near the well tank. Additionally, there were three separate areas in the garage that was wet. These areas are closer to the garage door, with one being right beside the garage door entrance. The time of my observation was approximately 7:30 pm.

I would like guidance on whether I should be concerned with additional water seepage into the basement and garage areas.

I appreciate your attentiveness. You can contact me at (704) 622-6982 or (704) 849-7379.

Sincerely,

Abbie Thornton

Installation 3

Finally, the owner of the company oversaw the 2nd reinstallation, and I did not have any additional issues with the drain. As you can see that a person's ego got in the way because I suggested that the drain was not deep enough. This caused their company money and labor and it caused me inconveniences and my time.

LETTER 6: Patio Enclosure – Deck Installation

(Honey Doer) - September 16, 2006

On February 21, 2006, I contracted with Honey-Doer to enclose my patio which was on the basement level. As a part of the enclosure, the upper deck was to become the roof of the patio. The contractor put a rubber membrane over the existing deck and added two drainage pipes that would move the water from the membrane. A new deck flooring was added on top of the membrane. The cost of this enclosure was $23,589.

Around April 2006, approximately 6-8 weeks later, I noticed that some of the slabs on the deck flooring had started to come loose and warp. On May 1, 2006, I wrote a letter to the owner regarding my concerns.

2135 Light Brigade Drive
Matthews, North Carolina 28105
May 1, 2006

Ron Frederick
Honey-Doer

Subject: Floating Deck

This is to inform you that another "slap" of wood on the deck has come loose. This slap is elevated or tilted upward.

This is the third instance of slabs on the deck coming apart. I am really concerned of the hazard that these "slaps" could cause, as well as the reliability of the deck structure itself.

It appears that after a heavy rain, these slabs are coming apart from the deck structure. I am bit concerned that this will be an on-going problem.

I would like to hear about some alternatives to rectifying this structure permanently.

Sincerely,

Abbie Thornton

Over the next 2-3 months, I made several efforts to contact the owner so the deck could be repaired. I left several voice messages, and he finally visited my home on August 5, 2006. At that time, he agreed to repair and/or replace the deck slabs. Another 4-6 weeks went by and I still did not hear from the owner.

On September 16, 2006, I wrote another letter to the owner detailing our conversations over the 5-6 months period.

2135 Light Brigade Drive
Matthews, North Carolina 28105
September 16, 2006

Ron Frederick
Honey-Doer
6100 Davidson Drive
Matthew, NC 28104

Subject: Floating Deck Issues

This memo is a follow-up to the numerous conversations we have had since the installation of the floating deck during March 2006. Below is a summary of those conversations:

- This is to inform you that another "slap" of wood on the deck has come loose. This slap is elevated or tilted upward. The water from the rain is not rolling off the deck, but is standing still under the "floating deck".
- This is the third instance of slabs on the deck coming apart. I am really concerned of the hazard that these "slaps" could cause, as well as the reliability of the deck structure itself.
- It appears that after a heavy rain, these slabs are coming apart from the deck structure. I am bit concerned that this will be an on-going problem.
- On August 5, 2006, you visited my home and we discussed alternatives to the standing water problem. We agreed that you would put a "slant" in the deck floor to allow the water to drain off properly. We also agreed that you would start work on repairing the deck the week of August 28th.
- After calling you inquiring as to why the work on the deck had not started, on August 30th, you left a voice mail message indicating that you had to finish up on another client and would not be able to start on the deck repair until the week of September 4th.
- I have left you voice messages for the last two weeks and have not received a response from you as of today.

I am enclosing pictures that were taken during July 2006 where the wood on the deck has already rotten due to the standing water. Slabs are continuing to come loose and are "warping". Screws in the wood have already rusted.

I would appreciate you contacting me at your earliest convenient so we can resolve the deck repair issue.

Sincerely,

Abbie Thornton

Death of Partner

By this time, I had become furious. The owner had a partner that had worked with him on the patio enclosure. I had been trying to contact him as well and was not getting a response either. I had left messages indicating that since I am not getting a response, I am assuming you all were DEAD.

A few days later, I received a call from a young lady regarding the message I had left on their voice mails. I told her the situation and indicated that I had been trying to contact the owner of the company, and his partner whom I found out was her dad. She indicated that her dad was found dead in Florida earlier in the year. I gave her my condolences regarding her dad.

Hospitalization of Owner
Also, she said that the owner of the company had been in the hospital for a while. The owner finally contacted me and indicated he had been bit by some poisonous insect while he was in the mountains and had to be hospitalized.

Nevertheless, he finally came to my home and repaired and or replaced the deck slabs.

LETTER 7: Roof Replacement
(Priority One) - August 12, 2011

I moved into my home at 2135 Light Brigade Drive July 2003. Over the years, there have been several storms and hurricanes causing wind and hail damage to my roof.

I noticed a few shingles had blown off my roof one day while mowing my lawn during April 2011. I asked a friend if he would replace the shingles that had been blown off the roof. Once he was able to get on the roof, he noticed that I had a lot of damage to several shingles.

I subsequently noticed leaks in the ceiling in the upstairs bathroom and master bedroom closet.

During June 2011, I contacted a roofing company, Priority One. Priority One came to my home and placed a tarp on the roof. I signed a work authorization, under the impression that work would start in the next 2-4 weeks. See documents below:

Work Authorization

FIRE ★ WATER ★ WIND ★ MOLD
704-841-7663
24 HOUR EMERGENCY RESPONSE

This is a Work Authorization Form:

Property Owner(s) / Insured(s): _____

Property Address: _____ City / Zip: _____

Home Phone: _____ Cell Phone: _____

Email: _____

Insurance Company: _____

Policy #: 33-6J-1481-4   Claim(s) #: 33 D633-S1D

___ I, the Property Owner, hereby confirm that I would like my Insurance Company to work directly with Priority 1 Restoration to resolve the Claims listed above, including any interior and exterior damage, as well as any repairs needed to secure or protect the Property.

___ I, the Property Owner, hereby authorize Priority 1 Restoration to perform all repairs outlined in the final insurance claim (scope of work).

___ I, the Property Owner, hereby authorize the Insurance Company to pay Priority 1 Restoration directly.

___ I, the Property Owner, will provide Priority 1 Restoration all necessary information for billing and reviewing purposes.

___ I, the Property Owner, agree that if the Insurance Company issues payment to me rather than to Priority 1 Restoration, I will pay Priority 1 Restoration immediately upon my receipt of funds.

___ I, the Property Owner, certify that no one else has been on my roof with the exception of _____.

___ I, this Property Owner, agree to give Priority 1 Restoration all necessary access to the property during Priority 1 Restoration's business hours for the purpose of inspection and repair (i.e., Lockbox).

___ I, the Property Owner, acknowledge that Priority 1 Restoration is providing concierge customer claim service in the good faith expectation of receiving all work to be performed in connection with the Claim. I recognize that these services represent a minimum value of $750. In the event Priority 1 Restoration and my Insurance Company cannot reach an agreement as to the terms for repair on this Claim, this contract will be terminated. I acknowledge that if I breach the terms of this agreement, I am to pay all mitigation, inspection, logistical, legal and any other fees incurred in connection with this Claim.

Referral Program ___ YES ___ NO   Referral Name: _____

Insured Signature: _____   Date: _____

State Farm Letter dated: July 7, 2011

State Farm Insurance Companies

State Farm Insurance Companies
1500 State Farm Blvd
P.O. Box 9024
Charlottesville, VA 22906-9024
888 736 2713;Fax 888 736 2711

July 7, 2011

Abbie Thornton
2135 Light Brigade Dr
Matthews, NC 28105 6413

RE: Claim Number: 33-D633-510
    Date of Loss: June 25, 2011

Dear Ms. Thornton:

Please find enclosed our estimate of repair as well as payment in the amount of $3,513.21, representing the actual cash value of repairs. This represents payment under Section I - Dwelling Coverage of your policy.

By the terms of your policy, the enclosed claim payment includes your mortgage company/lienholder as a payee.

The name appearing on this payment may not be familiar to you. Many mortgagees and lienholders use servicing agents to collect payments and handle other details of the lien for them. Since each mortgagee/lienholder has different procedures for endorsing such payments, we suggest you contact the office to which you make your payments and ask them what they require.

Please have the contractor of your choice review the estimate. Should you or your contractor have any questions concerning the estimate, please call us at the number listed below before any work is started.

To make a claim for Replacement Cost Benefits of your policy, simply return the enclosed Explanation of Building Replacement Cost Benefits form to us, along with the bills for repairs. Payment will then be issued to you for the actual cost of repairs, or $3,838.71, whichever is less. At our option, an inspection of these repairs will be made.

If you have any questions, please contact us.

Sincerely,

HOME OFFICES: BLOOMINGTON, ILLINOIS 61710-0001

Abbie Thornton
Page 2
July 7, 2011

Win Hunter (signature)
Win Hunter
Claim Representative
(888) 736-2713, extension 2448384

State Farm Fire and Casualty Company

Enclosures

Priority One Contract Document July 22, 2011

Priority 1 Restoration

PO Box 1021
Matthews, NC 28106
704-841-7663/ Fax 704-841-1060

Insured:	Abbie Thornton	Home:	(704) 849-7379
Property:	2135 Light Brigade Dr	Business:	(704) 622-6982
	Matthews, NC 28105		

Estimator: Authorization

Contractor:		Business:	(704) 841-7663
Company:	Priority 1 Restoration		
Business:	PO Box 1021		
	Matthews, NC 28105		

Claim Number: Policy Number: 33GJ08614   Type of Loss:

Date Contacted:	6/25/2011		
Date of Loss:	4/9/2011	Date Received:	6/25/2011
Date Inspected:	6/29/2011	Date Entered:	7/7/2011 11:29 PM

Price List: NCCL7X_JUL11
Restoration/Service/Remodel
Estimate: 2011-07-07-2329

X _(signed)_ 7/22/11   _(signed)_ 7/22/11

The signature on this contract reflects work authorization by party accepting responsibility for payment. Payment in full reflects customer is satisfied.

Should default be made in payment of this contract, charges shall be added from date thereof at a rate of one and one half percent per month (18%/annum) with a minimum charge of $2.00 per month, and if placed in the hands of an attorney for collection, all attorney's fees, legal filing fees shall be paid by customer accepting contract. Priority 1 Restoration LLC will have the right to supplement the Insurance Company in the event that additional work is needed due to unforeseen circumstances or material and labor increase over five percent (5%) from the date of the damage or if labor and materials exceed the original scope of loss. For the written warranty to become valid must be paid in full.

These repairs do not constitute a guarantee or warranty of adequacy, performance or condition of any structure, item or system connected to or adjacent to any item addressed in this contract.

-Please note: We will inspect decking and replace as needed: $50.00 per 4x8 sheet of plywood installed NOT INCLUDED IN TOTAL

Priority 1 Restoration asks that homeowner remove any items/furniture in area where work is being completed. Priority 1 Restoration cannot be held liable for damage to any items/furniture left in those areas. Homeowner releases Priority 1 Restoration of any liability associated with any damage to property left in those areas.

Priority 1 Restoration

PO Box 1021
Matthews, NC 28106
704-841-7663/ Fax 704-841-1060

2011-07-07-2329

Main Level

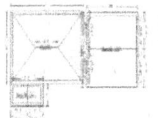 Roof1

2,883.69 Surface Area
341.33 Total Perimeter Length
94.60 Total Hip Length

28.84 Number of Squares
50.50 Total Ridge Length

DESCRIPTION	QNTY	REMOVE	REPLACE	TOTAL
1. Remove Tear off, haul and dispose of comp. shingles - 3 tab	28.84 SQ	44.38	0.00	1,279.92
2. Roofing felt - 30 lb.	30.33 SQ	0.00	26.36	799.50
3. Laminated - comp. shingle rfg - w/out felt	33.33 SQ	0.00	156.74	5,224.14
4. Remove Additional charge for high roof (2 stories or greater)	28.84 SQ	4.54	0.00	130.93
5. Additional charge for high roof (2 stories or greater)	33.33 SQ	0.00	10.98	365.96
6. Remove Additional charge for steep roof - 10/12 - 12/12 slope	28.84 SQ	17.69	0.00	510.18
7. Additional charge for steep roof - 10/12 - 12/12 slope	33.33 SQ	0.00	39.08	1,302.54
8. R&R Flashing - pipe jack	4.00 EA	5.67	23.69	117.44
9. R&R Continuous ridge vent - shingle-over style	32.00 LF	0.68	6.34	224.64
10. R&R Furnace vent - rain cap and storm collar, 5"	2.00 EA	8.63	39.32	95.90
11. R&R Chimney flashing - average (32" x 36")	1.00 EA	15.11	228.44	243.55
12. R&R Counterflashing - copper	61.00 LF	0.47	8.52	548.39
21. R&R Roof mount power attic vent	1.00 EA	20.15	248.68	268.83

Totals: Roof1 11,111.92

Priority 1 Restoration

PO Box 1021
Matthews, NC 28106
704-841-7663 V Fax 704-841-1060

Bathroom
Height: 8'

224.00 SF Walls
269.00 SF Walls & Ceiling
5.00 SY Flooring
28.00 LF Ceil. Perimeter

45.00 SF Ceiling
45.00 SF Floor
28.00 LF Floor Perimeter

DESCRIPTION	QNTY	REMOVE	REPLACE	TOTAL
13. Mask or cover per square foot	45.00 SF	0.00	0.31	13.95
19. Exhaust fan - Detach & reset	1.00 EA	0.00	139.83	139.83
14. Contents - move out then reset - Small room	1.00 EA	0.00	32.53	32.53
18. Mask and prep for paint - paper and tape (per LF)	28.00 LF	0.00	0.54	15.12
15. Protect contents - Cover with plastic	45.00 SF	0.00	0.18	8.10
16. Seal/prime the ceiling - two coats	45.00 SF	0.00	0.65	29.25
17. R&R Acoustic ceiling (popcorn) texture	45.00 SF	0.37	0.81	53.10

Totals: Bathroom 291.88

Total: Main Level 11,403.80

Line Item Subtotals: 2011-07-07-2329 11,403.80

Adjustments for Base Service Charges	Adjustment
Electrician	172.60
Total Adjustments for Base Service Charges:	172.60

Line Item Totals: 2011-07-07-2329 11,576.40

Priority 1 Restoration

PO Box 1021
Matthews, NC 28106
704-841-7663 V Fax 704-841-1060

Grand Total Areas:

224.00 SF Walls	45.00 SF Ceiling	269.00 SF Walls and Ceiling
45.00 SF Floor	5.00 SY Flooring	28.00 LF Floor Perimeter
0.00 SF Long Wall	0.00 SF Short Wall	28.00 LF Ceil. Perimeter
45.00 Floor Area	54.78 Total Area	224.00 Interior Wall Area
885.19 Exterior Wall Area	30.67 Exterior Perimeter of Walls	
1,883.69 Surface Area	28.84 Number of Squares	341.33 Total Perimeter Length
50.50 Total Ridge Length	94.60 Total Hip Length	

2011-07-07-2329

7/22/2011   Page: 4

40

Priority 1 Restoration

PO Box 1021
Matthews, NC 28106
704-841-7663/ Fax 704-841-1060

Summary for Dwelling

Line Item Total				11,403.80
Total Adjustments for Base Service Charges				172.60
Material Sales Tax	@	7.250% x	3,893.76	282.30

Replacement Cost Value   **$11,858.70**
Net Claim   **$11,858.70**

_____ 7/22/11
Authorization

State Farm Letter dated: July 23, 2011

State Farm Insurance Companies

State Farm Insurance Companies
1500 State Farm Blvd
P.O. Box 9024
Charlottesville, VA 22906-9024
888-736-2713 / Fax 888-736-2711

July 23, 2011

Abbie Thornton
2135 Light Brigade Dr
Matthews NC 28105-6413

RE: Claim Number: 33-D633-510
    Date of Loss: June 25, 2011

Dear Mr. Thornton:

Enclosed is a payment in the amount of $7826.87. Please refer to the following attachment(s) which outline(s) the basis for our payment:

Statement of Loss

Your policy includes several coverages available to you, and this payment is made under the following:

Section I Coverage A

Please call me if you have any questions.

Sincerely,

Benjamin F. Carr
Claim Representative
(888) 736-2713, extension 2448232 Fax # 888-736-2711

State Farm Fire and Casualty Company

Enclosure(s)

HOME OFFICES: BLOOMINGTON, ILLINOIS 61710-0001

STATEMENT OF LOSS

Insured: Abbie Thorton
Claim #: 33-D633-510

COVERAGE A - BUILDING
Limit of Liability

Description	Amount
Priority One estimate for repair	$ 11,858.70
Priority One temporary repairs	$ 481.38

Total A $ 12,340.08

COVERAGE B - OTHER STRUCTURES
Limit of Liability

Description	Amount
	$ -

Total B $ -

COVERAGE C - PERSONAL PROPERTY
Limit of Liability

Description	Amount

Total C $ -

COVERAGE D - LOSS OF USE
Limit of Liability

Description	Amount

Total D $ -

Comments/Supplements

Total A+B+C+D	$ 12,340.08
Plus Special Coverage	
Total Loss	$ 12,340.08
Less Depreciation - Cov. A	$ -
Less Depreciation - Cov. B	
Less Depreciation - Cov. C	$ -
Subtotal	$ 12,340.08
Less Deductible	$ 1,000.00
Less Prior Payments	$ 3,513.21
TOTAL	$ 7,826.87

Benjamin F. Carr Sr   7/23/2011
SIGNATURE   DATE

State Farm Check Number: 1 07 989282 J

Scheduling Concerns

On 7/27/2011 at 9:15am, I wrote the following email to Priority One regarding scheduling:

> *Good Morning Hollie:*
>
> *How are you? I called approximately an hour ago inquiring about the scheduling of the roof replacement. I have been told several times that Priority One will contact me when they have a date. It has been approximately one month since this process started. I understand that Priority One is unable to give me an exact date. However, I am aware that Priority One should be at least be in a position to give me a tentative timeframe to work with. Anything less than that is unacceptable.*
>
> *It has been mentioned that Priority One has had to fire some of their crew which is impacting the schedule. Nevertheless, an organization can only plan their existing resources. Based upon Priority One's current resources, what is a reasonable timeframe by which the roof repair can be scheduled and completed?*
>
> *There are other repairs that I am trying to schedule which is dependent upon the completion of the roof replacement.*
>
> *Thanks. I appreciate your attention.*
>
> *Abbie Thornton*
> *2135 Light Brigade Drive*
> *Matthews, NC 28105*

State Farm Letter dated: August 9, 2011

> State Farm Insurance Companies
>
> State Farm Insurance Companies
> 1500 State Farm Blvd
> P.O. Box 9024
> Charlottesville, VA 22906-9024
> 888-736-2713 Fax 888-730-0711
>
> August 9, 2011
>
> Abbie Thornton
> 3135 Light Brigade Dr
> Matthews, NC 28105-6413
>
> RE: Claim Number: 33-D633-510
> Date of Loss: June 25, 2011
>
> Dear Ms. Thornton:
>
> Enclosed is a payment in the amount of $481.38. This represents payment under Section I of your Homeowners Policy. This represents payment for the temporary repairs completed to your roof.
>
> Thank you for your cooperation in the handling of your loss.
>
> Sincerely,
>
> Win Hunter
> Claim Representative
> (888) 736-2713, extension 244-8384
>
> State Farm Fire and Casualty Company
>
> Enclosure
>
> ---
>
> CLAIM NO 33-D633-510   POLICY NO 33-GJ0861-4   LOSS DATE 06-25-2011   PAYMENT NO 1 07 737808 J
> Coverage Description   Amount COL/Line Pay Cd   DATE 08-09-2011
> MIN/PAID – Building $481.38 35/001   1   AMOUNT $481.38
>
> RETAIN STUB FOR RECORDS
> AUTHORIZED BY HUNTER, WIN
> PHONE (888) 736-2713
>
> REMARKS   Coverage A draft for temporary repairs
>
> HOME OFFICES: BLOOMINGTON, ILLINOIS 61710-0001

I subsequently reimbursed State Farm $481.38 due to a duplicate payment using check #7780 dated 9/21/2011.

Request for Refund

Approximately two month later, Priority One had not given me an estimated start date, nor were they responding to my inquiries regarding the start date. I wrote the following letter to the owners below requesting a refund of the money I had paid so far.

2135 Light Brigade Drive
Matthews, North Carolina 28105
August 12, 2011

Marc Skinner
Jennifer Skinner
Priority 1 Restoration and Contracting
1110 Technology Drive
Indian Trails, NC

Subject: Roof Repair – Claim Number 33D633-510 (Request for Refund)

On June 25, 2011, I contacted your Company regarding a leak in my bathroom that appeared to be the result of storm damage. Your Company responded timely and placed a "tarp" over an area as well as "boots" around the pipes.

On July 6, 2011, your Company met State Farm at my home while they were doing their review of the potential damage.

On July 15, 2011 (Friday), Ginger Howard visited my home to compare State Farm and Priority One estimates; as well as picked out the shingles for the roof repair. During this meeting, I was asked for the initial check that State Farm has sent to me for the roof repairs in the amount of **$3,513.21**. At that time, the check had not been endorsed by Well Fargo Bank.

> *According to Priority One Claim Process, step #6, "During this appointment the reconstruction phase will be scheduled with a member of our staff. *All exterior and interior reconstruction scheduling is weather permitting.*

On July 18, 2011 (Monday), I wrote a personal check #7719 in the amount of **$3,513.21** to Priority One and it was picked up on the same day by Ginger Howard.

On July 22, 2011, I visited your office and met with Ginger Howard to sign an updated version of your estimate so it can be sent to State Farm

During each of these encounters, I inquired concerning when or how soon you could replace and/or repair the roof. I was informed that you would need to check the schedule and get back with me.

Subsequent to this time, I have made numerous attempts to obtain a date or time frame as to when the roof will be replaced:
1. On July 27, 2011, I call your office inquiring about the scheduling of the roof repair and was told that someone would call me back shortly. I never received a

phone call. I subsequently sent an email to Hollie (Office Manager) on the same day and have not received a response from her.

2. July 31, 2011 – I left a voice mail in your general mailbox for Marc Skinner to give me a call. No response.
3. August 2, 2011 – I called your office and was put on hold for 6 minutes. Tracy indicated that the person that does the scheduling (appears to be Ginger Howard) was not answering her phone. She left a message for that person to call me. However, I never received a call. Nevertheless, Tracy thought that this person may have mentioned that it would probably be some time during the month of September 2011.
4. August 2, 2011 – I left a voice message on Ginger Howard, Operations Manager cell phone (919-771-7920) regarding the scheduling and asked her to give me a call. No response.
5. August 8, 2011 – I called your office and asked for a number to call Jennifer Skinner, Owner. I was told that they were not authorized to give me her number but was transferred to Jennifer Skinner's voice mail. I left a voice mail for Jennifer to call me. No response.

As of today, your Company has only incurred a total cost of **$481.38** related to the temporary repairs.

As of August 12, 2011, Priority One has not scheduled my repairs, and has not given me any kind of official indication as to when Priority One may complete the repairs.

As a result of the above, I am considering this contract void and would like to request a refund in the amount of $3,031.83. See details below:

Initial Payment	$ 3,513.21
Temporary Repairs	$ 481.38
Refund Amount	**$ 3,031.83**

The refund can be mailed to my address noted above.

Sincerely,

Abbie Thornton

CC: Atty. T. M. Todd

Certificate of Satisfaction

Within the next three weeks, Priority One completed the installation of my roof. Below is the certificate of satisfaction.

CERTIFICATE OF SATISFACTION/COMPLETION

Date: 8/29/11

I/We, Abbie Thornton the owner(s) of the property at the
(Name of Property Owner)

address indicated below, stated that the work completed in scope of work claim/policy# 33-D633-510
(Description of Work)

services provided by **Priority 1 Restoration** has been completed to our complete satisfaction.

Comments:

Abbie Thornton 9/2/2011
Customer Signature

2135 Light Brigade Dr
Address

Matthews, NC 28105
City, State and Zip Code

704-822-6982
Phone

Received by: _David_.

Note: Any omitted or defective items noted after this form is signed is covered by a separate Warranty issued by Priority 1 Restoration upon receipt of final payment.

LETTER 8: Sprinkler System Installation
(Water Saver Irrigation, Inc.) - August 2014

During the Spring of 2014, I contracted Water Saver Irrigation to install a sprinkler system in my front and side yard. I was given a two-year warranty on parts and labor.

During the month of July 2014, I noticed that water was "oozing" out of one of the sprinkler heads. I contacted the Water Saver Irrigation company to have them come repair the sprinkler head. I made three attempts to contact the owner regarding the issue I was experiencing with the sprinkler head. He indicated several times that he would be sending someone out to inspect it, but that did not happen after 2-3 weeks. I then wrote the following letter dated August 6, 2014 indicating my efforts.

Additionally, I was still under warranty and wanted to ensure I did my part in notifying the company on a timely basis.

2135 Light Brigade Drive
Matthews, NC 28105
August 6, 2014

Mr. Doug Viele
Water Saver Irrigation, Inc.
409 Chase Oaks Ct.
Waxhaw, NC 28176

Subject: Request for Service

I would like to go on record regarding my request to have a sprinkler head checked.

On July 19, 2014, I texted you indicating that water was "oozing" out of the sprinkler head beside the CPI Security sign. You indicated you would send someone out next week to check it.

On July 27, 2014, I texted again inquiring as to whether you sent anyone to my home last week to check out the "oozing" sprinkler head. You indicated that you would send someone out on Monday, July 28th.

I called you on August 1, 2014 and you indicated you would send someone out on Saturday, August 2, 2014.

As of today, August 6, 2014, no one has come to check out the "oozing" sprinkler head.

I trust that this is not an indication of the level of service your Company will be providing to its customers in the future.

Sincerely,

Abbie Thornton

After the owner received the letter, he scheduled a technician to come to my home and repair the sprinkler head. Any future concerns were addressed on a timely basis and the warranty period was honored each time there was a needed repair.

LETTER 9: Damaged Pipes
(Well Doctor) - March 2019

During the month of March 2019, it was noted that there was a busted pipe under my driveway that went from my well pump into my house. I contracted the Well Doctor to reroute a line from the well pump to the well tank in my basement. After inspecting the well tank which had been in the home for 30 years, it was recommended that I replace the well tank too, and I did.

A trench was dug alongside my driveway, then the concrete across my driveway was cut; and the trench continued towards the front of the house where the pipe went into the brick wall and was connected to the well tank in the basement. The pipes were in a "U" shape.

<u>Depth of Trench</u>
As the trench was being manually dug, I inquired as to whether it was being dug deep enough. I was concerned that if the ground got cold, the pipes may burst. Of course, the laborer indicated that it only needed to go down 5-6 inches. According to my research, the pipe should be buried a little deeper.

As the Laborers were putting the dirt over the pipes in the ground, I inquired as to whether they needed to pack the dirt down so that the rain would not wash the dirt away. They indicated that the rain would pack the dirt down. My lawn was at a "slant", so when it rains the water runs off at the slant. A few days later it rained, and the dirt was washed away from the buried pipes. I took pictures of this and sent to the Office Administrator to have someone come out and cover the pipe.

Leaky Tank
When the Technician installed the well tank, I questioned him as to whether he had tightened the bolts securely. He informed me that he had been doing this for a while and knew what he was doing. The next morning, I went to my basement to ensure there was not a leak coming from the tank, and realized the tank was leaking. I called the Technician and informed him the tank was leaking. He had to come back to my home and drain the tank so that he could tighten the bolts.

Busted pipes
After the new line and water tank were installed, I contacted the company that maintains my sprinkler system to have the system started up for the spring. This company wanted to charge me approximately $400-$500 to start-up the sprinkler system. I inquired as to why, and they indicated that they did not know if any sprinkler pipes needed to be repaired that may have been busted as the Well Doctor were installing the new line.

I contacted another company to start-up my sprinkler system. In the process of doing this, we found out there was a leak somewhere in the yard. It was determined that the Well Doctor laborers had cut into the Sprinkler System line and did not inform me before they covered the area back up. This cost me approximately $300 to get this repaired.

By this time, I was totally upset about the whole experience. I decided to write a review on Yelp regarding the above experience and rated Well Doctor with "one-star". The next day the owner of the company contacted me to make everything right. He agreed to reimburse me for the $300 I paid to repair the busted sprinkler pipe. Additionally, I was given a lifetime warranty on the installed pipes. See below:

PO Box 1420, Mount Pleasant, NC 28124
(704) 909.9258

Name of Purchaser: ABBIE THORNTON
Address of Property: 2135 LIGHT BRIGADE DR MATTHEWS NC 28105
Purchaser's Address: 2135 LIGHT BRIGADE DR MATTHEWS NC 28105

Product Purchased: BLACK POLY PIPE
Length of Warranty: LIFETIME
Installation Date: 3/26/19
Expiration Date: WILL NEVER EXPIRE

Warranty covers parts and labor and is transferable should the property be sold or transferred.

I updated my rating explaining how the owner had addressed my concern timely and what was done to make my situation whole again; and gave them a five-star rating. I sold my home February 2020 and passed this warranty onto the new owners.

PART III
REAL ESTATE

LETTER 10: Payoff of Principal on Loan
(Wells Fargo Amortization) - 2010 – 2011

During January 2010, I sent the following letter to Wells Fargo to apply funds in the amount of $6,360.58 towards the principal balance of my mortgage loan. See Letter 1 below:

2135 Light Brigade Drive
Matthews, NC 28105
January 5, 2010

Wells Fargo Home Mortgage
P. O. Box 11701
Newark, NJ 07101-4701

Subject: Loan Number 0265155226

I am enclosing a check in the amount of **$6,360.58** to be applied to principal for the following payment numbers as noted in the enclosed amortization schedule:

Payment Number	Principal Amount
2	$624.52
3	$627.05
4	$629.60
5	$632.16
6	$634.73
7	$637.31
8	$639.89
9	$642.49
10	$645.10
11	$647.73
Total	**$6,360.58**

Thank you.

Sincerely,

Abbie Thornton

Attachment: Amortization Schedule

After I received my next mortgage statement, I noticed that Wells Fargo had applied part of the $6,360.58 towards my February 2010 mortgage payment, and the remainder to the end of my mortgage loan. I wrote the following letter to point out their failure to apply the funds as requested in my original letter dated January 5, 2010. See letter 2 below:

2135 Light Brigade Drive
Matthews, NC 28105
January 16, 2010

Wells Fargo Home Mortgage
P. O. Box 11701
Newark, NJ 07101-4701

Subject: Loan Number 0265155226 – Principal Balance Adjustment Request

In a letter that was dated January 5, 2010, I requested that you apply a check in the amount of **$6,360.58** to the following payment numbers that are reflected in my current amortization schedule.

Payment Number	Principal Amount
2	$624.52
3	$627.05
4	$629.60
5	$632.16
6	$634.73
7	$637.31
8	$639.89
9	$642.49
10	$645.10
11	$647.73
Total	**$6,360.58**

Instead, you applied part of the amount above to my February 2010 payment. See attached "**Monthly Mortgage Statement**". I am requesting that you make an adjustment and apply the money as initially requested. All of the $6,360.58 should have been applied to the principal balance.

Please send me an updated amortization schedule. Thank you.

Sincerely,

Wells Fargo Home Mortgage subsequently made the necessary adjustments and applied the funds to the principal balances as requested.

During August 2011, approximately 17 months later I requested funds of $4,257.64 to be applied to the principal balance of my mortgage loan. This time I included the due date so that it would be clearer as to where the funds should be applied.

2135 Light Brigade Drive
Matthews, NC 28105
August 15, 2011

Wells Fargo Home Mortgage
Customer Services Department
P. O. Box 10335
Des Moines, IA 50306

Subject: Loan Number 0265155226

I am enclosing a check in the amount of **$4,257.64** to be applied to principal for the following payment numbers as noted in the enclosed amortization schedule:

Payment Number	Due Date	Principal Amount
21	September 1, 2011	702.43
22	October 1, 2011	705.29
23	November 1, 2011	708.15
24	December 1, 2011	711.03
25	January 1, 2012	713.92
26	February 1, 2012	716.82
Total		**$4,257.64**

Please send me an updated amortization schedule. Thank you.

Sincerely,

Abbie Thornton

This time, Wells Fargo Home Mortgage applied the funds correctly. This allowed me to pay my mortgage loan down by 20 months and I saved substantial amounts of interest.

LETTER 11: Retroactive Re-Assessment of Taxes

(Mecklenburg County Tax Collector) - May 24, 2016

During 2015, the Mecklenburg County Tax Collector Department decided to go back four (4) years and retroactively reassess homeowners' taxes from 2011 through 2014. As a result, the tax value of my home increased from $334,400 to $357,500. This was an increase of $23,100 that I was retroactively accessed taxes upon.

I appealed to the Mecklenburg County Board of Equalization and Review, and a decision was made to reduce my property value from $357,500 to $350,500 instead on June 19, 2015. This resulted in a $16,100 increase of taxes that were retroactively reassessed after four years.

See email below:

6/20/2015   Appeal for 2135 Light Brigade Dr. - Parcel 215-251-95

From: Murray, Candace <Candace.Elbert@mecklenburgcountync.gov>
To: ATITACS <ATITACS@AOL.COM>
Subject: Appeal for 2135 Light Brigade Dr. - Parcel 215-251-95
Date: Fri, Jun 19, 2015 12:39 pm

Hello Ms. Thornton,

I have reviewed your appeal of 2135 Light Brigade Dr. and I am recommending a value reduction from $357,500 to $350,500 for tax years 2011 to 2014. If this is acceptable, please acknowledge by returning this message with a statement of acceptance. This action will move your case to the consent agenda of the Board of Equalization for Mecklenburg County. You will receive a formal letter from the Board of Equalization within 2 to 3 weeks after the hearing. If you acknowledge the proposed value, there will not be a need to attend the meeting.

Thank you,

[signature]

Candace Murray
Mecklenburg County
Real Property Appraiser
County Assessor's Office
700 E. Stonewall St Suite 203
Charlotte, NC 28202
980-314-4353

Please take a moment to rate my customer service *Assessor's Office Customer Service Survey*

On March 8, 2016, a year after Mecklenburg County performed the retroactive reassessment of taxes, I subsequently received a letter from my mortgage company, CitiMortgage. CitiMortgage indicated I was delinquent in paying my property taxes from 2011 to 2014. I responded to CitiMortgage with the following letter.

63

Letter 1:

2135 Light Brigade Drive
Matthews, NC 28105
March 11, 2016

CitiMortgage, Inc. – 0059307
P.O. Box 961247
Ft. Worth, TX 76161-0247

Subject: Supplemental Taxes Parcel 215-251-95

On August 6, 2015, the Mecklenburg County Board of Equalization and Review made a decision to reduce my property value from $357,500 to $350,500 after reviewing my appeal. A notice of this decision was sent to me in letters dated September 4, 2015, (see Attachments A-D)

The initial tax bills based on the **$357, 500** values are noted below. (see Attachments E-H for the initial bills).

Year	Value Before Appeal	Tax
2011	$357,500	$ 258.51
2012	$357,500	$ 252.88
2013	$357,500	$ 261.77
2014	$357,500	$ 261.77
		$1,034.93

I recalculated the tax bill for the following years based on the reduced property value of **$350,500**. See Attachments E-H.

Year	Value After Appeal	Tax	Date Paid	Check#
2011	$350,500	$ 180.17	09/07/2015	9098
2012	$350,500	$ 176.24	11/02/2015	9141
2013	$350,500	$ 182.45	12/01/2015	9156
2014	$350,500	$ 182.45	12/31/2015	9157
		$ 721.31		

I have received the following refunds from the Mecklenburg County Tax Department indicating that, "*This check is a refund of Property Taxes paid to Mecklenburg County.*" See Attachments I-J.

Check Date	Check#	Tax Bill Number	Amount
01/27/2016	4259672	0002003995-2015-2013-0000-00	$182.45
03/08/2016	4276570	0002003995-2015-2014-0000-00	$182.45

Sincerely,

Abbie Thornton

Attachments

Approximately 3 weeks later, I had to write another letter to CitiMortgage explaining that I had paid the supplemental taxes and the amounts they were basing the taxes on had changed due to the appeal. I then had to send documentation from the Mecklenburg Tax Collectors' Office verifying I did not owe any taxes. See letter below:

Letter 2

2135 Light Brigade Drive
Matthews, NC 28105
March 28, 2016

CitiMortgage, Inc. – 0059307
P.O. Box 961247
Ft. Worth, TX 76161-0247

Subject: Supplemental Taxes, Parcel 215-251-95, Loan Number 1122934195

This memo is in response to your letter dated March 8, 2016 regarding supplemental taxes owed, noted below:

Year	Value Before Appeal	Tax
2011	$357,500	$ 258.51
2012	$357,500	$ 252.88
2013	$357,500	$ 261.77
2014	$357,500	$ 261.77
		$1,034.93

I appealed the retroactive increase in taxes during the years noted above. Mecklenburg County Tax Assessor subsequently adjusted the tax value of my property. I paid the taxes on the readjusted value for the years noted above in 2015.

I am attaching a statement from the Tax Collector's Office dated **March 28, 2016** indicating that my current balance is **$0.00**.

Sincerely,

Abbie Thornton

Attachments

Even after the Tax Collector's Office had given the documentation on March 28, 2016 indicating that my tax bill was zero (0), the Tax Assessor's office subsequently mailed me a revised bill on 3/29/2016 that was still incorrect. See letter below:

Letter 3

2135 Light Brigade Drive
Matthews, NC 28105
May 24, 2016

Mecklenburg County Tax Collector
P.O. Box 71063
Charlotte, NC 27272

Subject: Supplemental Taxes Parcel 215-251-95

On August 6, 2015, the Mecklenburg County Board of Equalization and Review made a decision to reduce my "retroactive property value increase" from $357,500 to $350,500 after reviewing my appeal. A notice of this decision was sent to me in letters dated September 4, 2015.

The initial tax bills based on the **$357, 500** values are noted below.

Year	Value Before Appeal	Tax
2011	$357,500	$ 258.51
2012	$357,500	$ 252.88
2013	$357,500	$ 261.77
2014	$357,500	$ 261.77
		$1,034.93

I recalculated the tax bill for the following years based on the reduced property value of **$350,500**. The original value was **$334,400**, and the total increase was **$16,100**. I submitted payment for the following years as noted below:

Year	Value After Appeal	Tax	Date Paid	Check#
2011	$350,500	$ 180.17	09/07/2015	9098
2012	$350,500	$ 176.24	11/02/2015	9141
2013	$350,500	$ 182.45	12/01/2015	9156
2014	$350,500	$ 182.45	12/31/2015	9157
		$ 721.31		

As a result of me paying the tax bill prior to the revised billed being generated and mailed to me, your system generated a refund check for 2013 and 2014 since there was no indication than an amount was due.

I have received the following refunds from the Mecklenburg County Tax Department indicating that, "*This check is a refund of Property Taxes paid to Mecklenburg County.*"

Check Date	Check#	Tax Bill Number	Amount
01/27/2016	4259672	0002003995-2015-2013-0000-00	$182.45
03/08/2016	4276570	0002003995-2015-2014-0000-00	$182.45

On March 8, 2016, I received a letter from my mortgage company (CitiMortgage) indicating I was delinquent in the taxes for the 2011, 2012, 2013 and 2014 years.

March 11, 2016: I visited the Mecklenburg County Tax Office to understand what was happening with my tax bills. At this time, someone (Tiffany and Supervisor) took notes and indicated that would be passing the information on the Real Estate to make the corrections.

March 28, 2016: I made a second visit to Mecklenburg County Tax Office to follow-up regarding the corrections to my account. I was informed that Kim Deal had made an adjustment to my accounts, and that I would be receiving revised bills.

I received revised bills dated March 29, 2016. However, these bills were also incorrect, and did not take into consideration that I had already paid my taxes in full for 2011 and 2012.

April 6, 2016: I made a third visit to Mecklenburg County Tax Office to discuss the revised bills being incorrect and they had already been paid in full for 2011 and 2012. At this time, I spoke with Julia Aten and Lisa Westmoreland. It was suggested that I be refunded my payments for 2011 and 2012; and that my account be cleared and be re-billed all over again for the 4 years.

As of today, I have not received any updates on the status of the resolution. I would certainly appreciate some assistance in getting this matter resolved.

Sincerely,

Abbie Thornton

Summary

I made a final visit to the Mecklenburg County Tax Collector's Office on May 24, 2016, with the above letter to be delivered personally to the Director over the Department. I requested to meet with the Director on May 24, 2016. Suddenly, some individuals were pulled out of an all-day meeting to address and resolve my issues on the spot.

As you can see from the string of correspondences, it took over a year for the Mecklenburg County Tax Department to clear up my account.

LETTER 12: Giving the Gift of a Home

(My Home) - December 2019

On June 27, 2017, I wrote this letter to a friend of mine suggesting he give his wife of 30 years, the gift of a home. I shared this letter with some colleagues of mine. See sample of letter below:

2135 Light Brigade Drive
Matthews, NC 28105
June 27, 2017

Mr. & Mrs. Buyers
123 Main Street
Charlotte, NC 28200

Subject: **30 Year Wedding Anniversary**

As you are contemplating what gift to buy your bride of 30 years, consider giving the "Gift of a New Home". Renew your commitment to her by unlocking the door on December 10, 2017 and carrying her across the threshold of her new home into another 30 years.

A man's job defines who he is; but a woman's home defines who she is. It is her castle; it is where she entertains her friends; it is where she nurtures her children and grandchildren; it is where the family comes together; and it is where she provides benevolence to her husband.

I will work with you to prepare your existing home to sale; as well as assist you in finding the perfect "new" home for your bride of 30 years.

Please let me know when you are available to have a conversation.

Sincerely,

Abbie Thornton
Abbie.thornton@kw.com
704-622-6982

During February 2019, I listed my home with a high-end realty company. I am a licensed realtor but did not have the time to deal with the sale of my home myself. It was recommended that I do some upgrades and remodeling. I had the main level of the home remodeled and upgraded. The home had not sold by the end of the listing contract which covered a 6-month period. I decided not to renew my listing with this realty company. Instead, I listed my own home August 1, 2019 through Keller Williams Realty, and I was the selling realtor.

After listing my own home, I was reading the book "**The Power of Your Subconscious Mind**". I have had this book for over 20 years, and I re-read this book on a regular basis. There is a section in the book that talks about how to become successful in buying and selling a home specifically. I started reciting the following after I listed my home on August 1, 2019.

"Infinite intelligence attracts to me the buyer for my home who wants it and who prospers in it. This buyer is being sent to me by the creative intelligence of my subconscious mind which makes no mistakes. This buyer may look at many homes, but mine is the only one they want and will buy, because they are guided by the infinite intelligence within them. I know the buyers are right, the time is right, and the price is right. Everything about it is right. The deeper currents of my subconscious mind are now in operation bringing both of us together in divine order. I know that it is so."

I realized that what you are seeking is also seeking you. Whenever you want to sell a home or property, there is always someone who wants what you have to offer.

On 8/31/2019, I held an Open House at my home at 2135 Light Brigade Drive, Matthews, NC. I had approximately 20 individuals to attend the Open House. I requested everyone to sign-in upon entry into the house. Over the next several months, I had several showings and a few unacceptable offers.

During the month of December 2019, I had put these huge "red bows" on the front of my house and smaller ones on the three brick columns across the front of my yard as my Christmas decorations. I said to myself that I was wrapping my house as a gift to a lucky family.

On December 20, 2019, I received an offer on my home for the full list price at that time. My home was this family's Christmas gift.

I later had a conversation with the Buyer's Realtor, and she indicated that her buyers had attended my Open House in August 2019. She also said that she had shown them several homes, but they kept coming back to my home.

I went back to check my sign-in list from the Open House and noted that the buyers were the last couple that had signed my sheet. They were from Garner, NC and was looking to relocate to Charlotte, NC because the husband's company was moving to Charlotte. The family had 4-5 kids and the wife was home schooling the kids. They wanted each kid to have their own bedroom, and my home would accommodate that need, as well as provide a separate area for their home schooling and an in-ground indoor pool.

We closed on the house February 6, 2020.

LETTER 13: Home Appraisal Challenge
(Samaritan's House Inc.) - January 2020

I received an offer on my home December 2019 at the list price. An appraisal was requested by the lending institution, and the appraisal came back at $400,000.

The realtor contacted me recommending I drop the price down to $400,000 or provide documentation to substantiate the sales price. The County of Mecklenburg reassessed tax value of the home was $527,500. After me contesting Mecklenburg County on the $527,500, the tax value was dropped to $501,200. See letters below and the associated documents:

2135 Light Brigade Drive
Matthews, NC 28105
January 6, 2020

Charlene Thompson
BHHS Carolinas Realty
3420 Toringdon Way, Suite 200
Charlotte, NC 28277

Subject: Contested Appraisal: 2135 Light Brigade Drive

The purpose of this memo is to contest the appraisal that was completed 01/06/2020 by Eugene L. Poore (Samaritan) on property at 2135 Light Brigade Drive at a value of **$400,000.**

1. On January 23, 2019, I received a notification from Mecklenburg County Assessor's Office that my property was reassessed at a value of $527,000. I contested this value and requested an Appeal.
   - See document: *2135 Light Brigade Drive - 2019 Real Estate Assessed Value.pdf*
2. On February 1, 2019, I had an appraisal performed on the property by J. Hanes Walker & Associates. The appraisal came back at $420,000.
   - See document: *2135 Light Brigade Drive Appraisal 02.01.2019.pdf*
3. The consistent feedback from potential buyers of the property was that updates/upgrades needed to be made to the property; and they did not want to make the updates themselves.
4. During the April-June 2019 timeframe, the property was taken off the market to make upgrades to the house. The main level was upgraded at a cost of approximately $30,000. See documents:
   - *Est_18423_from_Carolina_Quality_Flooring__Cabinets_10584 (1).pdf*
   - *Inv_18467_from_Carolina_Quality_Flooring__Cabinets_11356 (5).pdf*
   - *Inv_18665_from_Carolina_Quality_Flooring__Cabinets_12600 CT*
   - *Inv_18832_from_Carolina_Quality_Flooring__Cabinets_12600 CT*
5. On August 3, 2019 the property was relisted under Keller Williams Realty at a list price of $487,000. The CMA that was used to determine the list price is attached. See document:

- 2135 Light Brigade - CMA Report Aug 03 2019

6. On September 18, 2019 and after the appeal, Mecklenburg County Assessor's Office reduced the tax value to $501,200. See documents:
    - Meck County Tax Assessor Appeal Decision 09.18.2019 page 1.pdf
    - Meck County Tax Assessor Appeal Decision 09.18.2019 page 2.pdf

The assumption the Appraisal made indicating, ("*The Subject was on the market 999 with a list price ranging from 449,900 to 527,00 with no sales occurring suggests and indicates the $449,900 sales was too high to induce a sale.*"); is misleading and inconclusive. Several offers were made during this time, and none were acceptable to the seller. Additionally, the home has been upgraded and the tax value has increased which has contributed to the changes in the prices over time.

Note: This home was also appraised 1/17/2012 (eight years ago) at a value of $375,000.

Sincerely,

Abbie Thornton

CC: Sabra Romeo, BIC Keller Williams Balllantyne

Document 1: 2019 Real Estate Assessed Value

Mecklenburg County
Assessor's Office
PO Box 31127
Charlotte, NC 28231
Website: MeckReval.com
Phone: 980-314-4226

THIS IS NOT A BILL

THORNTON ABBIE
10655 PARKHOUSE LN
CHARLOTTE NC 28269-1445

Date: January 23, 2019

Notice of 2019 Real Estate Assessed Value

Parcel Number	Property Address	Market Value	Deferred Amount*	Assessed Value
21525195	3135 LIGHT BRIGADE DR MATTHEWS	$527,500	$0	$527,500

Dear Property Owner,

Mecklenburg County has reappraised all property as required by North Carolina General Statute (NCGS)105-286. Pursuant to Chapter 105, Subchapter II of the NCGS, the assessed value above is the market value of your property as of January 1, 2019. Every property owner is entitled to a property visit and observation to verify the accuracy of characteristics that are on record for the property.

Here are your options:

1. If you agree with the assessed value above, STOP. You do not need to do anything further. Please keep this information for your records.

   OR

2. If you have questions or disagree with your assessed value follow these steps:
   - ✓ Visit **MeckReval.com** and enter the parcel number above to review your assessment
   - ✓ You can request an informal review of your assessed value online at **MeckReval.com** or by completing the enclosed Informal Review Form within **30 days** of receiving this Notice of 2019 Real Estate Assessed Value
   - ✓ If you wish to skip the informal review, you can file a Formal Appeal request with the Board of Equalization and Review (BER) by May 20, 2019. Please see the back of this page for more information about filing an appeal
   - ✓ You can contact the County Assessor's Office at AssessorQuestions@MeckNC.gov or call 980-314-4226

Important Dates:

January, 2019 – Notice of 2019 Real Estate Assessed Value is sent to all County property owners. You may review your assessed value and property characteristics online at **MeckReval.com**

May 20, 2019 – BER Adjournment/Deadline for Formal Appeal of Assessed Value to be filed

Page 1 of 4

Document 2: Appraisal 02.01.2019

FEATURE	SUBJECT	COMPARABLE SALE # 1	COMPARABLE SALE # 2	COMPARABLE SALE # 3
Address	2135 Light Brigade Dr Matthews, NC 28105-6413	13709 Jonathans Ridge Rd Mint Hill, NC 28227-7501	2231 Annabel Ct Matthews, NC 28105-0460	15022 Ron Allen Ct Mint Hill, NC 28227-7649
Proximity to Subject		1.18 miles NE	0.67 miles NW	1.07 miles NE
Sale Price	$	$ 375,000	$ 397,000	$ 445,000
Sale Price/Gross Liv. Area	sq.ft. $	$ 121.36 sq.ft.	$ 184.39 sq.ft.	$ 128.24 sq.ft.
Data Source(s)		MLS #3416426;DOM 76	MLS #3397925;DOM 52	MLS #3367678;DOM 24
Verification Source(s)		Doc #33195-951;CMLS/Tax Recor	Doc #32989-530;CMLS/Tax Recor	Doc #32714-820;CMLS/Tax Recor
VALUE ADJUSTMENTS	DESCRIPTION	DESCRIPTION +(-) $ Adjustment	DESCRIPTION +(-) $ Adjustment	DESCRIPTION +(-) $ Adjustment
Sales or Financing Concessions		ArmLth Conv;5000	ArmLth VA;5270	ArmLth Conv;0
Date of Sale/Time		s12/18;c11/18	s09/18;c07/18	s05/18;c04/18
Location	N;Res;	N;Res;	N;Res;	N;Res;
Leasehold/Fee Simple	Fee Simple	Fee Simple	Fee Simple	Fee Simple
Site	1.27 ac	28750 sf +3,050	16988 sf +4,400	21344 sf +3,900
View	N;Woods;	N;Res; 0	N;Res; 0	N;Res; 0
Design (Style)	DT2;Traditional	DT1;Ranch 0	DT2;Traditional	DT2;Traditional
Quality of Construction	Q3	Q3	Q3	Q3
Actual Age	30	25 0	14 -3,200	17 -2,600
Condition	C3	C3	C3	C3
Above Grade	Total Bdrms Baths	Total Bdrms Baths	Total Bdrms Baths	Total Bdrms Baths
Room Count	9 5 3.0	7 4 2.1 +10,000	7 5 3.1 -10,000	7 4 3.1 -10,000
Gross Living Area	3,272 sq.ft.	3,090 sq.ft. +3,640	2,415 sq.ft. +17,140	3,470 sq.ft. -3,960
Basement & Finished	1562sf1562sfwo	0sf +15,620	1314sf1103sfwo +4,590	0sf +15,620
Rooms Below Grade	1rr0br1.0ba2o	0rr0br0.0ba0o +10,000	0rr0br0.0ba0o +10,000	0rr0br0.0ba0o +10,000
Functional Utility	Average	Average	Average	Average
Heating/Cooling	FWA;CA	FWA;CA	FWA;CA	FWA;CA
Energy Efficient Items	None	None	None	None
Garage/Carport	2ga2dw	2ga2dw	2ga2dw	3ga3dw -10,000
Porch/Patio/Deck	CovPch;Deck	CovPch;Deck	Pat;Pch;Deck 0	Pch;Deck 0
Fireplaces	2 Fireplaces	1 Fireplace +2,000	1 Fireplace +2,000	1 Fireplace +2,000
Appliances/Upgrades/Updating	Average	Average	Average	Average
Fence Extras, Guest Hse	Pool/Fence	None 0	None 0	None 0
Net Adjustment (Total)		☒ + ☐ - $ 44,310	☒ + ☐ - $ 24,930	☒ + ☐ - $ 4,960
Adjusted Sale Price of Comparables		Net Adj. 11.8 % Gross Adj. 11.8 % $ 419,310	Net Adj. 6.3 % Gross Adj. 12.9 % $ 421,930	Net Adj. 1.1 % Gross Adj. 13.1 % $ 449,960

☒ did ☐ did not research the sale or transfer history of the subject property and comparable sales. If not, explain

My research ☐ did ☒ did not reveal any prior sales or transfers of the subject property for the three years prior to the effective date of this appraisal.
Data Source(s) CoreLogic
My research ☒ did ☐ did not reveal any prior sales or transfers of the comparable sales for the year prior to the date of sale of the comparable sale.
Data Source(s) CoreLogic
Report the results of the research and analysis of the prior sale or transfer history of the subject property and comparable sales (report additional prior sales on page 3).

ITEM	SUBJECT	COMPARABLE SALE #1	COMPARABLE SALE #2	COMPARABLE SALE #3
Date of Prior Sale/Transfer			05/08/2018	
Price of Prior Sale/Transfer			$385,000	
Data Source(s)	CoreLogic	CoreLogic	CoreLogic	CoreLogic
Effective Date of Data Source(s)	02/02/2019	02/02/2019	02/02/2019	02/02/2019

Analysis of prior sale or transfer history of the subject property and comparable sales See attached sale history addendum

Summary of Sales Comparison Approach   A thorough search was made to find home sales considered more similar to the subject (with similar GLA, lot/view, condition and ammenities) however none were found within 12 months via MLS within the subject subdivision. The Appraiser has chosen the best and only applicable sales from the general area and adjusted accordingly. All comparable are the most recent and similar sales available. All sales are appropriately adjusted for all value influencing dissimilarities. All were fee simple estates and unaffected by common amenities. Due to the lack of availability of more similar recent sales - adjustments may exceed normal guidelines or exceed 1 mile from the subject. Sales are arranged in weighted order with most weight and credence placed on the sales requiring least "gross" adjustments ie: comps 1,2,3 receiving most credence and gradually less each sale thereafter. Listings 7, 8 and 9 are provided as guidance for comparing inventory. The Appraiser made an exhaustive search to find sales requiring less adjustments however these provided as deemed best available.

Indicated Value by Sales Comparison Approach $ 420,000

Indicated Value by: Sales Comparison Approach $ 420,000   Cost Approach (if developed) $ 432,302   Income Approach (if developed) $

Sales Comparison Approach is given most credence as income and cost data is not applicable. Appraiser has used a digital signature in compliance with USPAP.

This appraisal is made ☒ "as is", ☐ subject to completion per plans and specifications on the basis of a hypothetical condition that the improvements have been completed, ☐ subject to the following repairs or alterations on the basis of a hypothetical condition that the repairs or alterations have been completed, or ☐ subject to the following required inspection based on the extraordinary assumption that the condition or deficiency does not require alteration or repair.   See Statement of Limiting Conditions.

Based on a complete visual inspection of the interior and exterior areas of the subject property, defined scope of work, statement of assumptions and limiting conditions, and appraiser's certification, my (our) opinion of the market value, as defined, of the real property that is the subject of this report is
$ 420,000   , as of   02/01/2019   , which is the date of inspection and the effective date of this appraisal.

Document 3:
Est_18423_from_Carolina_Quality_Flooring__Cabinets_10584 (1)

Carolina Quality Flooring & Cabinets
3358 Smith Farm Rd
Matthews, NC 28104
(P) 704-821-4444 * (F) 704-821-1914

Estimate

Date	Estimate #
4/4/2019	18423

Name / Address
Berkshire Signature Properties
21024 Catawba Ave
Cornelius, NC 28031

Ship To
2135 Light Brigade Dr.
Matthews, NC 28105
LOCK BOX 1947

Customer Contact

Rep
MK

Description	Qty	Rate	Total
60" AW Vanity		657.79	657.79T
Granite Top		485.00	485.00T
Mecklenburg Sales Tax		7.25%	1,673.61

The undersigned guarantor has executed this agreement and personally guarantees payment of the account jointly and severally. In the event the account is placed with collection applicant agrees to pay reasonable attorney fees.
50% down. Balance upon completion.

Quote Accepted By: _____ $30,804.40

We look forward to working with you on this project.

Page 2

Document 4:

Inv_18467_from_Carolina_Quality_Flooring__Cabinets_11356 (5)

Carolina Quality Flooring & Cabinets
3358 Smith Farm Rd, Matthews, NC 28104
(P) 704-821-4444 (F) 704-821-1914

Invoice

Date	Invoice #
4/11/2019	18467

PAID 06-07-2019

Bill To
Abbie Thornton
10555 Parkhouse Ln
Charlotte, NC 28269

Ship To
2135 Light Brigade Dr
Matthews, NC 28105
LOCK BOX 1947

P.O. No.	Terms	Rep
		MC

Description	Qty	Rate	Amount
60" AW Vanity		657.79	657.79T
Luna Pearl Granite Top		485.00	485.00T
Carpet Starstruck #730 Ivory (Back Bedroom)		590.15	590.15T
Freight charge		80.00	80.00
6 LB Pad		92.50	92.50T
Installation of Carpet		150.00	150.00
Synchrony charge		-226.86	-226.86

Thank you - We appreciate your business.

Subtotal	$26,437.38
Sales Tax (7.25%)	$1,485.87
Total	$27,923.25
Payments/Credits	-$27,923.25
Balance Due	$0.00

Page 2

Document 5:
Inv_18665_from_Carolina_Quality_Flooring__Cabinets_12 600 CT

Carolina Quality Flooring & Cabinets
3358 Smith Farm Rd, Matthews, NC 28104
(P) 704-821-4444 . (F) 704-821-1914

Invoice

Date	Invoice #
5/15/2019	18665

Bill To
Abbie Thornton
10555 Parkhouse Ln
Charlotte, NC 28269

Ship To
2135 Light Brigade Dr
Matthews, NC 28105
LB 1947

P.O. No.	Terms	Rep
		MC

Description	Qty	Rate	Amount
Freendo Regal Series 2 Handle Lavatory Faucet	1	49.00	49.00T

Thank you - We appreciate your business.

Subtotal	$49.00
Sales Tax (7.25%)	$3.55
Total	$52.55
Payments/Credits	$0.00
Balance Due	$52.55

Document 6:

Inv_18832_from_Carolina_Quality_Flooring__Cabinets_12 600 CT

Carolina Quality Flooring & Cabinets
3358 Smith Farm Rd, Matthews, NC 28104
(P) 704-821-4444 (F) 704-821-1914

Invoice

Date	Invoice #
6/5/2019	18832

Bill To
Abbie Thornton
10555 Parkhouse Ln
Charlotte, NC 28269

Ship To

P.O. No.	Terms	Rep
		MC

Description	Qty	Rate	Amount
Plumbing		820.00	820.00

Thank you - We appreciate your business.

Subtotal	$820.00
Sales Tax (7.25%)	$0.00
Total	$820.00
Payments/Credits	$0.00
Balance Due	$820.00

Document 7: CMA August 3, 2019

atitacs@aol.com
Ofc Ph: 704-622-6982

Subject Property: 2135 Light Brigade Drive, Matthews   August 03, 2019

Summary of Comparable Listings

This page summarizes the comparable listings contained in this market analysis.

Active Listings

Address		Price	Beds	Bth F	Bth H	Ttl HLA	$/SqFt	List Date
2135 Light Brigade Drive			4	4	0	4834	102.81	
7916 Greylock Ridge Road		$449,000	5	3	1	5,018	$89.48	06/10/2019
1214 Ilsemont Place #25		$584,899	5	3	1	4,895	$119.49	03/29/2019
1241 Manicott Drive		$635,000	5	3	1	4,895	$129.72	05/31/2019
	Averages:	$556,300	5.0	3.0	1.0	4,936	$112.90	

Closed Listings

Address		Price	Beds	Bth F	Bth H	Ttl HLA	$/SqFt	Contract Date
2135 Light Brigade Drive			4	4	0	4834	102.81	
2011 Shannon Bridge Lane		$425,000	5	3	1	4,147	$102.48	07/01/2019
10511 Olde Irongate Lane		$505,000	5	4	0	4,656	$108.46	06/28/2019
1306 Manicott Drive		$615,000	5	3	1	5,031	$122.24	05/01/2019
	Averages:	$515,000	5.0	3.3	0.7	4,611	$111.06	

Incomplete Listings

Address		Price	Beds	Bth F	Bth H	Ttl HLA	$/SqFt	Contract Date
2135 Light Brigade Drive			4	4	0	4834	102.81	
2135 Light Brigade Drive		$497,000	4	4	0	4,834	$102.81	
	Averages:	$497,000	4.0	4.0	0.0	4,834	$102.81	

	Low	Median	Average	High	Count
Comparable Price	$425,000	$505,000	$530,128	$635,000	7
Adjusted Comparable Price	$425,000	$505,000	$530,128	$635,000	7

Document 8: Meck County Tax Assessor Appeal Decision 09.18.2019 page 1

Mecklenburg County Assessor's Office
P.O. Box 31127
Charlotte, NC 28231-1127
www.MeckNC.gov/AssessorsOffice

BER-REL-D

September 18, 2019

ABBIE THORNTON
10555 PARKHOUSE LN.
CHARLOTTE NC 28269-1445

SUBJECT: NOTICE OF DECISION - CASE 19-BER-96382

Dear Taxpayer:

On August 21, 2019, the Mecklenburg County Board of Equalization and Review received evidence and heard testimony regarding your appeal. Based on the evidence and testimony, and in due consideration of all applicable laws, the Board made the following decision for tax year 2019 effective for January 1, 2019 (based on the 2019 general reappraisal year).

COUNTY IDENTIFICATION/DESCRIPTION OF PROPERTY UNDER APPEAL

PARCEL ID:	21525195
Description of Property:	L4B M32-318
Property address (if applicable):	2135 LIGHT BRIGADE DR MATTHEWS, NC
Assessed Valuation under appeal:	$527,500
Decision of the Board:	DECREASE/$501,200

You may appeal the Board's decision by filing a timely appeal with the North Carolina Property Tax Commission ("Commission"). The appeal **must** be received by the "Commission" or postmarked by the U.S. Postal Service within thirty (30) days from the mailing of the County Board's Notice of Decision. A copy of this Notice of Decision *must* accompany your appeal to the "Commission". The "Commission" will not accept electronic copies (i.e. Fax, email, etc.).

To file an appeal with the North Carolina Property Tax Commission, you may 1) Go online to the Department of Revenue's website at https://www.ncdor.gov/documents/av-14-north-carolina-property-tax-commission-notice-appeal-and-application-hearing and complete the Notice of Appeal and Application for Hearing (Form AV-14) **or** 2) Send a signed letter (notice of appeal) stating the grounds for the appeal and identifying the property being appealed. After receiving the signed letter, copies of the Notice of Appeal and Application for Appeal (Form AV-14) will be provided by our office to the taxpayer to complete and return to the "Commission" **within 30 days.**

The appeal from the County Board's Notice of Decision may be filed by (a) Property owner or party having an ownership interest in the property, (b) attorney representing the property who is licensed to practice law in North Carolina, (c) if the property owner is a business entity (i)officer, (ii)manager or member-manager, if the business entity is a limited liability company, (iii) employee whose income is reported on IRS Form W-2, if the business entity authorizes the representation in writing, or (iv)owner of the business entity, if the business entity authorizes the representation in writing and if the owner's interest in the business entity is at least twenty-five (25%), (d) a general partner, if the owner is a partnership, (e) trustee, if the property owner is a trust, and (f) executor/executrix, if the property owner is an estate. **If the property owner is a business entity and wishes to authorize a representative as defined in (c) above, form AV-63 must be complete and provided to the "Commission" within 30 days of the date the property was first appealed.**

When prepared, the Notice of Appeal and Application for Hearing (Form AV-14) **or** the signed letter (notice of appeal) with a copy of board's decision letter, must be postmarked (see above) and mailed to the following address: **North Carolina Property Tax Commission, P.O. Box 871, Raleigh, NC 27602** The "Commission" staff is available to answer questions by calling **(919) 814-1129**

(See Reverse)

PEOPLE ✦ PRIDE ✦ PROGRESS ✦ PARTNERSHIPS

Document 9: Meck County Tax Assessor Appeal Decision 09.18.2019 page 2

The "Commission" rules require that you also send a copy of your notice of appeal to the county tax administrator/assessor and to the county attorney.

Sincerely,

Christina Lantis

Clerk, Board of Equalization and Review

Send your appeal documents to:

North Carolina Property Tax Commission
PO Box 871
Raleigh, NC 27602
Commission Phone Number: (919) 814-1129

In addition, send copies of your Notice of Appeal to both the County Assessor and the County Attorney:

Mecklenburg County Assessor's Office 3205 Freedom Dr., Suite 3500 Charlotte, NC 28208	Robert Adden RUFF, BOND, COBB, WADE & BETHUNE, L.L.P. 831 E. Morehead St., Suite 560 Charlotte, NC 28202

After having to provide all the above documentation, the lender and buyers were satisfied that the list price was appropriate. We closed on the home on February 6, 2020.

PART IV
LEGAL RESOLUTION

LETTER 14: Cease and Desist Order
(Straight Arrow Construction) - September 19, 2007

During March 2007, I contracted with Straight Arrow Construction to enclose my swimming pool for $48,728. The work started May 1, 2007. See Proposal below:

Straight Arrow Construction
Monroe, North Carolina
704.777.9170

To: Abby Thorton

PROPOSAL

Work is proposed as follows:
Construct pool house over existing pool.
Housing is as follows:

1. Frame construction
2. Engineered full span scissor truss
3. Brick veneer
4. 12 sliding glass windows
5. Two full glass 4 ft. entrance doors with screens
6. 6 skylights as per roof plan (Gable glass custom fit to openings)
7. Lights placed so as to fully illuminate pool area
8. Concrete areas added to existing pad at ground level
9. Footings as required by code
10. 30-year shingles to match existing house color
11. Exterior trim to match existing house
12. Washable vinyl panels on interior walls
13. All phases of construction performed to state codes

Complete building time estimated at four to six weeks pending inspection time and weather factors.

Payment Schedule

Payment Description		Amount
First Payment – Truss, permits, masonry materials, masonry and footing labor	5/1/07	$7,500.00
Second Payment – Framing and building dry in	(6/1/07) 5,000.00	$7,500.00
Third Payment – Windows, skylights, and electrical work	(6/1/07) 7,400.00	$12,400.00
Fourth Payment – Exterior brick, trim, interior, and electrical finish	7/14/07	$5,500.00
Balance upon completion	8/10/07 — 5,000.00	$3,828.00
Crew Labor – Week One (6/15/07)		$3,000.00
Crew Labor – Week Two		$3,000.00
Crew Labor – Week Three 7/00/07		$3,000.00
Crew Labor – Week Four 7/13/07		$3,000.00
Total		$48,728.00

3/27/07
3/27/07

As the work commenced, I made the following payments.

Date	Check#	Amount
May 1, 2007	5795	$ 7,500.00
June 3, 2007	5838	$15,000.00
June 15, 2007	5851	$ 4,900.00
June 15, 2007	5855	$ 3,000.00
June 23, 2007	5860	$ 3,000.00
June 30, 2007	5863	$ 3,000.00
June 30, 2007	5864	$ 5,500.00
July 13, 2007	5884	$ 3,000.00
August 10, 2007	5913	$ 2,000.00
	Total	$46,900.00

I noticed that as the money began to dwindle, the work dwindled also. The contractor kept mentioning that they were running out of money. I re-emphasized what the contract amount listed for the enclosure, and that amount was the maximum that I would be paying.

Nevertheless, they were on time each week to ensure I paid them. I withheld $1,828 until the job was completed. Of course, this never happened. After I withheld the $1,828, limited work was being done if at all. Then the work stopped altogether. After a few weeks, I wrote my first letter requesting that they complete the pool enclosure by September 30, 2007, and request the final electrical inspection. See letter below:

2135 Light Brigade Drive
Matthews, NC 28105
September 19, 2007

John Vineyard
Straight Arrow Construction
2516 Brickyard Road
Monroe, NC 28110

Dear John:

This is a follow-up to the voice mail I left you on Sunday requesting the completion of the pool enclosure by September 30, 2007. I noticed that as of today, there has been no additional work done. I would like to have the final building and electrical inspections on the pool as soon as feasible.

Below is a listing of some obvious items that I could visually see that needs to be completed.
- Interior Trim
- Exterior finish (trim, caulking, etc.)
- Exterior painting
- Install windows (4)
- Remove paint from skylights (6). Be sure to cover pool with plastic before removal to ensure paint does not fall into pool.
- Back window screen needs to be installed securely
- Repair damage concrete on front of building, as well as fill in gaps between brick and existing concrete
- The concrete finish near the French door entrance close to pool pump is "slopped" too low causing water build-up when pool is used
- Repair chain-linked fence
- Place wooden fence back into place
- The concrete pad that was around the light post need to be replaced.
- Remove all excess material after completing job
- Etc.

I have kept my part of the contract and have paid you according to the schedule that you highlighted in the agreement. I would appreciate you keeping your part of the agreement by completing the pool enclosure. We are in the 5th month of the construction, and I do not want to go into another month. I appreciate your attention.

Sincerely,

Abbie Thornton

After sending the above letter, I did not immediately receive a response. The following letter was to request that the Electrician do a final electrical inspection.

2135 Light Brigade Drive
Matthews, NC 28105
October 5, 2007

John Vineyard
Straight Arrow Construction
2516 Brickyard Road
Monroe, NC 28110

Subject: Electrical Inspection

Would you please ask the Electrical Contractor to request a final electrical inspection on the pool enclosure?

Thank you.

Abbie Thornton

Cc: Bob Leckerman, Design Developers

After the contractor decided, they were not going to do any more work because the money had run out, I requested that they remove their tools from my property. See letter below:

2135 Light Brigade Drive
Matthews, NC 28105
November 22, 2007

John Vineyard
Straight Arrow Construction
2516 Brickyard Road
Monroe, NC 28110

Dear John:

I would appreciate you removing all of your tools and equipment from the property. Thanks. I appreciate it.

Sincerely,

Abbie Thornton

North Carolina Licensing Board Claim

The following letter represents my initial contact with the NC Licensing Board to file a claim against the contractor.

2135 Light Brigade Drive
Matthews, NC 28105
December 3, 2007

North Carolina Licensing Board for General Contractors
3739 National Drive, Suite 225
Raleigh, NC 27612

Subject: Complaint against General Contractor - Design Developers Contractor ID# X37835

On May 2, 2007, building permit #B1763186 for parcel #215-251-05 was granted to Design Developers (Bob Leckerman Contractor) for the enclosure of my pool. As of today, and seven (7) months later, the project has not been completed, and it appears that the general contractor has abandoned the project construction.

The contract in the amount of **$48,728** stated that the completion time estimates would be four to six weeks depending on weather. As we are aware, the weather has been dry, hot and pleasant in the state of North Carolina over the last several months.

On November 30, 2007, I noticed that the ceiling of the building which had been painted white was beginning to turn black and the nails that were exposed through the plywood had already rusted. I am assuming that either mildew is already beginning to buildup, or the "tar" from the shingles is bleeding through the plywood. In either case, I am seriously concerned about the viability of the construction of the pool enclosure.

It appears that the contractor did not use the appropriate type of paint for a construction of this nature, which is in violation of the building codes.

I am additionally concerned that we have an individual that is licensed as a contractor that is as negligible, unethical, and would provide unacceptable construction to the general public. It is of my opinion that this individual should not be associated with the North Carolina Licensing Board for General Contractors.

Below is a listing of obvious exposures, construction concerns and damages that I would like to report to the Licensing Board:
- Mildew build-up in ceiling
- Rusted nails
- Exterior of building was not painted
- Tacky patching of broken concrete inside and outside of building
- No gutters installed for proper water drainage
- Hill at back of building has not been "graded" to ensure it does not wash away
- Damaged chain-linked fence
- Damage to lawn landscape
- Broken concrete top covering electrical wire
- Light bulbs missing from exterior light fixtures

Over the last few months, I have had to constantly call and write the contractor and/or foreman requesting that the pool enclosure be completed. The work has been somewhat sporadic after my prompting; however it has not been completed.

I have enclosed photos that were taken on November 28, 2007 showing the current state of the construction.

I am currently in the process of obtaining other individuals to correct some of the issues noted above.

Sincerely,

Abbie Thornton

Cc: Russ Fisher, Mecklenburg County Building Inspector

Response from North Carolina Licensing Board

On December 4, 2007, the North Carolina Licensing Board for General Contractors responded to my complaint and provided me the necessary form to complete to file a complaint. See letter below:

Michael F. Easley, Governor
Carl E. Worsley, Jr., Chairman

North Carolina
Licensing Board for General Contractors

Post Office Box 17187
Raleigh, North Carolina 27619-7187
919/571-4183

December 4, 2007

Ms. Abbey Thornton
2135 Light Brigade Drive
Matthews, NC 28105

Re: Filing a Complaint

Dear Ms. Thornton:

Thank you for your inquiry regarding filing a complaint with the Board. Please find enclosed a complaint form. Should you choose to file a complaint, please complete the form in its entirety, have it notarized and return it to our office with supporting documentation.

Listing more than one contractor on the complaint form will result in your complaint form being returned. List the exact name on the complaint form that the contractor conducted business.

Should you have any questions, please give me a call at (919) 571-4189.

Sincerely,

Susan Dixon
Complaint Administrator

Enclosures

Design Developers Complaint

I subsequently found out that the building permit had been obtained by Design Developers and not by the company (Johnny A. Vineyard d/b/a Straight Arrow Construction) I had signed the contract with. Additionally, Design Developers indicated that the total cost of the construction was under $30,000 so they could obtain a permit. See follow-up letter to the North Carolina Licensing Board for General Contractors below.

2135 Light Brigade Drive
Matthews, NC 28105
December 6, 2007

North Carolina Licensing Board for General Contractors
c/o Susan Dixon, Complaint Administrator
Post Office Box 17187
Raleigh, NC 27619

Subject: Complaint against General Contractor - Design Developers Contractor ID# X37835

On December 3, 2007, I submitted a written complaint to your office concerning the above contractor. At the time, I was not aware this company was not properly licensed.

For clarity, my contract was signed with Straight Arrow Construction (John Vineyard). Design Developers obtained the building permit for the enclosure of the swimming pool.

I have subsequently been informed by the Mecklenburg County Building Inspector (Russ Fisher) that the building permit was obtained fraudulently. Design Developers indicated that the cost of the project was $29,700 to obtain the permit.

Enclosed are the following documents:
- Notarized Complaint Form
- Complaint Letter dated December 3, 2007
- Contract Proposal
- Copies of Canceled Checks (9)
- Lowe's Delivery Document

Sincerely,

Abbie Thornton

I completed and submitted the following complaint form from the North Carolina Licensing Board of Contractors.

Date: December 6, 2007

COMPLAINT AGAINST: Design Developers
Person, Partnership or Corporation (circle one)
4028 Bannockburn Place, Ste G, Charlotte   NC   28211
Street, Route #   City   State   Zip
(704) 492-0002   Robert (Bob) Leckerman
Telephone (day/eve)   Individual to contact

LOCATION OF PROJECT: 2135 Light Brigade Drive
Street, Lot No., Directions to job site, etc.
(Parcel 215-251-05)
Matthews   Mecklenburg
City   County

1. Please provide a brief description of the project (type of construction, i.e., dwelling, utility, highway, commercial building):
   Enclosure of an existing swimming pool at my home.

2. What is the cost of the project? $ 48,728.00

3. Please list the name(s), address, and telephone number of individuals, firms or businesses who have contracted with the respondent for the construction of this project:
   John A. Vineyard, Straight Arrow Construction   (704) 777-9170
   2516 Brickyard Road   Telephone
   Monroe   NC   28110
   City   State   Zip

4. Please provide the name and telephone number of the firm/individual who received bids for this project, if applicable:
   John A. Vineyard, Straight Arrow Construction, 704-777-9170

5. Was this project awarded to respondent by an architect, engineer or government agency? If so, please list the names and telephone number of the firm and/or principals involved with the project.
   No   (   )
                                                   Telephone

6. Have building permits or other permits been applied for or issued for this project? If so, name the issuing county or municipal inspections department or authority.
   Yes. Permit # B1763186 was issued by Mecklenburg County on 5/2/07

7. Please list the date (or approximate date) when work commenced on this project: May 7, 2007

8. List other individuals or subcontractors we may contact for additional information about this project:
   John A. Vineyard   2516 Brickyard Road, Monroe, NC 28110   704-777-9170
   Name   Address   Telephone

   Name   Address   Telephone

Abbie Thornton
Name of Person Completing this Form   Signature

2135 Light Brigade Drive Matthews NC 28105 (704) 849-7379
Address   City   State/Zip Telephone

The following letter dated December 11, 2007 is a notification from the North Carolina Licensing Board for General Contractors that they received my complaint.

Michael F. Easley, Governor
Carl E. Worsley, Jr., Chairman

North Carolina
Licensing Board for General Contractors

Post Office Box 17187
Raleigh, North Carolina 27619-7187
919/571-4183

December 11, 2007

Ms. Abbie Thornton
2135 Light Brigade Drive
Matthews, NC 28105

Re: Design Developers
 Complaint File No. 07C550

Dear Ms. Thornton:

This letter is to notify you that your complaint has been received, processed and assigned to a field investigator. During the investigation process the Raleigh office will be unable to assist you. Therefore, please refer all questions or inquiries regarding your complaint to the assigned Field Investigator. For your convenience contact information is provided below.

Kenneth B. McCombs
Central Piedmont Field Investigator
P. O. Box 17187
Raleigh, NC 27619
(704) 933-5554 – Office Phone

Sincerely,

Susan Dixon
Complaint Administrator

Follow-up on Complaint Status with Licensing Board

Several months had gone by and I had not heard from the Licensing Board of General Contractors. So, I sent the following letter inquiring on the status of the complaint.

2135 Light Brigade Drive
Matthews, NC 28105
May 13, 2008

North Carolina Licensing Board for General Contractors
3739 National Drive, Suite 225
Raleigh, NC 27612

Subject: Complaint File No. 07C550 - Design Developers

On December 3, 2007, I file a complaint against Design Developers. It was my understanding that the case was presented to the Board on April 4, 2008.

I am writing to obtain a status on the results of the Board hearing.

Sincerely,

Abbie Thornton

Response from Licensing Board – Injunction against Design Developer

The North Carolina Licensing Board of General Contractors responded back on May 21, 2008 and indicated that the Board's review committee agreed to seek an injunction against Design Developers for practicing general contracting without a license. See letter below.

Michael F. Easley, Governor
Carl E. Worsley, Jr., Chairman

North Carolina
Licensing Board for General Contractors

Post Office Box 17187
Raleigh, North Carolina 27619-7187
919/571-4183

May 21, 2008

Ms. Abbie Thornton
2135 Light Brigade Drive
Matthews, NC 28105

Re: Design Developers
Complaint File No. 07C550

Dear Ms. Thornton:

On May 15, 2008, our office received your letter regarding the complaint you filed against Design Developers. On April 10, 2008, the Board's review committee agreed to seek an injunction against Design Developers for allegedly practicing general contracting without a license. Once the matter has been resolved in Wake County Superior Court, our office will notify you in writing.

Should you have any questions, please give me a call at (919) 571-4189.

Sincerely,

Susan Dixon
Complaint Administrator

The following document is the "Notice of Review Committee Decision" related to Design Developers being unlicensed. On April 10, 2008, the Committee met and decided to continue the case until the next Review Committee meeting.

Review Committee
North Carolina
Licensing Board for General Contractors

NOTICE OF REVIEW COMMITTEE DECISION

In the matter of:)
)   UNLICENSED
)
DESIGN DEVELOPERS,   )
)   File No(s).   07C550
)
Respondent.   )

TAKE NOTICE that on the 10th day of April, 2008, at its regularly-scheduled quarterly Review Committee meeting or at a special meeting, the Review Committee ("Committee") of the North Carolina Licensing Board for General Contractors ("Board") met and considered the complaint(s) filed with the Board on the 10th day of December, 2007, regarding the above-named licensee or unlicensed contractor. By this Notice, after giving due consideration to the complaint(s) and the preliminary evidence submitted to and/or gathered by the Board during its investigation of the complaint(s), Respondent and Complainant(s) are hereby notified of the decision of the Review Committee.

Unless specified otherwise, the Committee convened for the purposes of considering this matter consisted of the following members:

        Carl E. Worsley, Jr., Board Member
        Mark D Selph, Secretary-Treasurer
        Carson Carmichael, III, General Counsel

Pursuant to 21 North Carolina Administrative Code ("NCAC") 12.0701(b)(3), the Review Committee is specifically delegated with the responsibility of determining, prior to a full-scale hearing, whether or not a charge of violating North Carolina General Statute ("N.C.G.S.") section 87-11(a), is unfounded or trivial. Upon receipt and review of all preliminary evidence, the Review Committee shall recommend to the Board that: (1) the matter be presented to the full Board for a hearing and determination on the merits of the charges, regardless of whether the alleged violations are admitted or denied; (2) in those instances where the alleged violations are admitted as true by the Respondent, the Board accept the Respondent's admission of guilt and order the Respondent not to commit in future the specific act or acts admitted by him to have been violated and, also not to violate any of the acts of misconduct specified in N.C.G.S. §87-11 at any time in the future; (3) the alleged violations be dismissed as unfounded or trivial; (4) the Board refer the matter to another agency for consideration in those instances where it is determined that the Board is without jurisdiction to discipline the alleged conduct; or, (5) the Board continue this matter where additional investigation is needed or additional time is warranted for corrective measures, prior to rendering a decision regarding any of the above issues. Pursuant to 21 NCAC 12 .0701(b)(3), the decision of the Review Committee is **FINAL**.

The Review Committee took the following action with respect to the complaint filed in this matter:

____ Dismissed the charges against the Respondent Contractor;
Review Committee found no probable cause to conduct a disciplinary hearing.

____ Found probable cause to conduct a disciplinary hearing to determine whether Respondent and/or Respondent's Qualifying Party violated N.C.G.S. §87-11(a) and agreed to send Respondent, Respondent's Qualifying Party and Complainant(s) a formal Notice of Administrative Hearing as to when, where, and what time the hearing would be held. The Administrative Hearing shall be held and a determination made by the Board on the merits of the charges(s) in accordance with the substantive and procedural requirements of the provisions of 21 NCAC 12.0800 and N.C.G.S. §87-11 as provided by 21 NCAC 12.0701(b)(6)(C).

(To be set forth in more detail in the Notice of Hearing in Pre-Hearing statement.)

____ **Reprimanded Respondent.** If Respondent does not wish to accept the reprimand, then Respondent may request a hearing before the Board pursuant to the provisions of 21 NCAC 12.0818.

____ With Respondent's consent, agreed to accept Respondent's Admission of Violation/Guilt in lieu of conducting a disciplinary hearing.

(Respondent will receive an Admission of Violation to execute.)

____ By service of this Notice, agreed to refer the complaint, along with the entire contents of the investigative file, to the appropriate agency with jurisdiction:

Agency to which referred: _____, or.

__XX__ **Other: The Review Committee decided to continue this case until the next Review Committee meeting.**

cc: Kenneth B. McCombs, Field Investigator
Abbie Thornton, Complainant(s)

On July 14, 2008, I received a call from an Attorney indicating they wanted to pull Johnny A. Vineyard into this case since I had signed the contract with him.

Several months had gone by and I had not heard anything from the Review Committee of the NC Licensing Board for General Contractors. The following is a letter dated February 1, 2009, that I wrote requesting a status on the case.

2135 Light Brigade Drive
Matthews, NC 28105
February 1, 2009

North Carolina Licensing Board for General Contractors
Post Office Box 17187
Raleigh, NC 27619-7187

Subject: Complaint File No. 07C550 - Design Developers

On July 14, 2008, I received a call from Attorney Cathy Plaut indicating that the complaint against Design Developers would be continued to include John Vineyard of Strait Arrow Construction in the case.

I am writing to obtain a status on where we are concerning the injunction against Design Developers for allegedly practicing general contracting without a license.

Sincerely,

Abbie Thornton

On February 4, 2009, the North Carolina Licensing Board of General Contractors responded and indicated that the Board agreed November 2008 to enter an injunction against Design Developers and have filed a complaint against Johnny A. Vineyard d/b/a Straight Arrow Construction. See letter below:

Michael F. Easley, Governor
Carl E. Worsley, Jr., Chairman

North Carolina
Licensing Board for General Contractors

Post Office Box 17187
Raleigh, North Carolina 27619-7187
919/571-4183

February 4, 2009

Ms. Abbie Thornton
2135 Light Brigade Drive
Matthews, NC 28105

Re: Design Developers
Complaint File No. 07C550

Dear Ms. Thornton:

Today, our office received your letter regarding the complaint you filed against Design Developers. On November 20, 2008, the Board's review committee considered the complaint filed against Design Developers and agreed to seek an injunction. The complaint has been forwarded to our attorney Cathy Plaut. Once the injunction has been entered I will forward you a copy.

Our office has filed a complaint against John Vineyard and Strait Arrow Construction (08C347) and we are currently investigating that complaint.

Should you have any questions, please give me a call at (919) 571-4189.

Sincerely,

Susan D. Sullivan
Complaint Administrator

Cease and Desist Order

After approximately three (3) months, the North Carolina Licensing Board of General Contracts issued a "Cease and Desist" order for Johnny A. Vineyard. See the six pages of the "Consent Order" below.

NORTH CAROLINA

WAKE COUNTY

IN THE GENERAL COURT OF JUSTICE
SUPERIOR COURT DIVISION
09 CVS 5080

NORTH CAROLINA LICENSING)
BOARD FOR GENERAL CONTRACTORS,)
)
    Plaintiff,)
)   CONSENT ORDER
v.)
)
JOHNNY A. VINEYARD d/b/a STRAIGHT)
ARROW CONSTRUCTION,)
)
    Defendant.)

The undersigned Superior Court Judge, having reviewed the signatures of the parties to this document, makes the following findings of fact, conclusions of law, and orders accordingly:

FINDINGS OF FACT

1. Plaintiff, the North Carolina Licensing Board for General Contractors, is an agency created under Chapter 87 of the North Carolina General Statutes. Its principal offices are located in Raleigh, North Carolina, within the boundaries of Wake County.

2. Defendant is a citizen and resident of Union County, North Carolina.

3. Plaintiff is charged with regulation and enforcement of the practice of general contracting within the State of North Carolina. G.S. §87-13.1 provides that Plaintiff has standing to seek injunctive relief against unlicensed contractors who are building projects such that they are required to be licensed under G.S. §87-1.

4. G.S. §87-1 requires that any person, firm or corporation who undertakes any building project where the cost of the undertaking is in excess of $30,000 be licensed unless

it is built for the builder's own use. G.S. §87-13 forbids the practice of general contracting in North Carolina without proper licensure.

5. Defendant is not now and never has been the holder of a valid license or certificate of renewal of license to practice general contracting in North Carolina.

6. On March 27, 2007, Defendant contracted with Abbie Thornton to construct a pool house in Matthews, North Carolina for a cost of $48,728.00.

7. The parties agree and stipulate to the above findings of fact and agree to be bound by the terms of this Consent Order.

CONCLUSIONS OF LAW

1. This Court has jurisdiction over the parties and subject matter to this action.

2. This Court has examined the signatures of the parties, and the parties are bound by all of the stipulations contained herein.

3. This Board has standing under G.S. §87-13.1 to seek this injunctive relief.

4. This Order is enforceable by the contempt powers of this Court, including the imposition of fines and/or imprisonment in the event of contempt of this Order.

IT IS ORDERED, ADJUDGED AND DECREED as follows:

1. That the Defendant be enjoined from the practice of general contracting in North Carolina until such time, if ever, that she is properly licensed.

2. That the costs of this action be taxed against Defendant and that Defendant forward a certified check or money order for court costs (Superior Court filing fee and Sheriff's Service fee) in the amount of $125.00 to Bailey & Dixon, LLP, c/o Cathleen M. Plaut, P.O. Box

-3-

1351, Raleigh, NC 27602, within ten days of service of this signed Consent Order upon Defendant;

3. That the Defendant comply with all provisions set forth in G.S. §87-1 and following, as required by law.

This the 12th day of _May_, 2009.

_____
Ronald L. Stephens
Superior Court Judge
Wake County

-4-

WE CONSENT:

Consent to entry of the foregoing is hereby acknowledged.

N.C. LICENSING BOARD FOR GENERAL CONTRACTORS

By: _____
Mark D Selph
Secretary/Treasurer
N.C. Licensing Board for General Contractors
Post Office Box 17187
Raleigh, NC 27619

NORTH CAROLINA
WAKE COUNTY

I certify that the following person personally known to me appeared before me this day, acknowledging to me that he voluntarily signed the foregoing document for the purpose stated therein and in the capacity indicated.

Sworn to and subscribed before me by Mark D Selph

this the 7th day of _May_, 2009.

_____
Brenda Spence
Notary Public

Brenda Spence
Printed Name of Notary

My Commission Expires: 1/17/2013

*BRENDA SPENCE
NOTARY
Comm. Exp.
1-17-2013.
PUBLIC
WAKE COUNTY, NC*

BAILEY & DIXON, L.L.P.

By: _____
Cathleen M. Plaut
Attorneys for North Carolina
Licensing Board for General Contractors
Post Office Box 1351
Raleigh, NC 27602-1351

NORTH CAROLINA
WAKE COUNTY

I certify that the following person personally known to me appeared before me this day, acknowledging to me that she voluntarily signed the foregoing document for the purpose stated therein and in the capacity indicated.

Sworn to and subscribed before me by Cathleen M. Plaut

this the 7th day of May, 2009.

_____
Notary Public

Patricia A. Young
Printed Name of Notary

My Commission Expires: 10-14-2011

-6-

_____
Johnny A. Vineyard

STATE OF NORTH CAROLINA
UNION COUNTY

I certify that the following person personally known to me appeared before me this day, acknowledging to me that he voluntarily signed the foregoing document for the purpose stated therein and in the capacity indicated.

Sworn to and subscribed before me by Johnny A. Vineyard

this the 5 day of MAY, 2009.

_____
Notary Public

Guido Palmaccio
Printed Name of Notary

My Commission Expires: April 8, 2013

```
GUIDO PALMACCIO
Notary Public
Mecklenburg County
North Carolina
My Commission Expires Apr 8, 2013
```

-7-

CERTIFICATE OF SERVICE

The undersigned attorney for Plaintiff certifies that on this day the foregoing Consent Order was served upon the Defendant in this action by depositing a copy thereof in the United States mail, postage prepaid, and addressed as follows:

Mr. Johnny A. Vineyard
1406 Olive Branch Road
Monroe, NC 28110

This the 15 day of May, 2009.

_____
Cathleen M. Plaut

Conclusion: It took approximately two (2) years to put this contractor out of business.

LETTER 15: Landscaping
(Intrinity Landscaping, LLC) - June 2014

Signed Proposal

On June 1, 2014, I contracted with Intrinity Landscaping to install a "sod" grass in my yard. I mistakenly dated the contract for 6/1/2015 instead of 6/1/2014.

On June 28, 2014, I made final payment for the installation of the sod. See receipt below:

From: noreply <noreply@mobilepay.bankofamerica.com>
To: atitacs <atitacs@aol.com>
Subject: Receipt from INTRINITY LANDSCAPING
Date: Sat, Jun 28, 2014 6:56 pm

6/28/2014 11:53:24 PM (UTC)

INTRINITY LANDSCAPING
9331 BARKRIDGE RD
MINT HILL, NC 28227, US
7045265457

Response
Success

Transaction Type	Credit Sale
Terminal ID	4326748
Merchant ID	908848
Stan	36
AuthID	09657G
Invoice Number	439167
AVS Response	5Dgt Zip Match Only
CVV Response	Match
Card Last Four	Visa 9527
Description	Final payment for sod
Amount	$4,237.50
Tax	$0.00
Tip	$0.00
Total	$4,237.50

Signature

Thank You For Your Business

Bank of America Merchant Services

Privacy Policy

Memo to the File: 07/19/2014

MEMO TO THE FILE
July 19, 2014

The purpose of this memo is to document some observations while my sod was being installed on June 27 and June 28, 2014.

- On June 27, 2014 a delivery truck of sod was made to my home at 2135 Light Brigade Drive, Matthews, NC 28105
- As I am sitting in my bedroom looking out the window, I notice that Nick Sangella brought another pallet of sod to my house on June 27, 2014. I became suspicious as to why he would be bringing sod to my home when Super Sod just made a delivery. I suspect he did not order the amount of sod that I paid for (approximately 9500 sq. ft.)
- As the day progressed on June 27 and 28, the individuals installing the sod had thrown aside several dead or dried out pieces of sod.
- I asked if I could just put those pieces in my back yard where I had some bare spots and they said yes.
- There were at least two (2) wheel barrels of sod that had been put to side because the installers concluded these were not good pieces to install. I put these pieces in my backyard in those bare spots.
- Close to the end of the installation on June 28th, the installer realized they did not have enough sod to complete the installation of my yard. So, they went and got those pieces from my back yard and pretty much just patched them in the remainder area to be covered with sod.
- I also noted that there were areas that had been prepared for sod, which was never completed. This was along the left "outer-side" of my driveway coming into my yard. Additionally, there was an area on the right side of my house that had been prepared and was not covered because they ran out of sod.
- I thought that the sod would eventually spread and did not make a big deal out of it.

However, after seeing the condition of my yard after 12 days, I concluded that the majority of the sod installed was of poor quality. A lot of this was evident by the dead sections through out my yard. The areas where there was some greenery also had dead sections intertwined.

I am also wondering as to why Nick had to bring another pallet of sod to my house on the back of his truck.

Sincerely,

Abbie Thornton

Request to Replace Dead Sod

Letter #1

2135 Light Brigade Drive
Matthews, NC 28105
July 19, 2014

Nick Sagnella
Intrinity Landscaping
9331 Barkridge Road
Mint Hill, NC 28227

Subject: Replacement of Super-Sod's St. Augustine Sod

The purpose of this memo is to document our understanding regarding the replacement of the sod installed on June 28, 2014 that was initially "dead".

On 6/21/14, an advanced payment was made in the amount of $4,237.50 for the installation of St. Augustine sod.

On 6/28/14, a final payment was made in the amount of $4,237.50 upon completion of the sod installation.

During the installation, there were several sod pieces that appeared to have been dried out; however, it was indicated that these pieces still had seed, and would be revitalized after a good rain. After approximately five days of heavy rainfall the sod pieces were still dead.

On 7/2/14, I inform you that there were over 75 areas in the yard where the grass was dead. You indicated on 7/3/14 that you had already contacted Super Sod and it would be some time next week before you are able to get the sod.

On 7/9/14, I inquired as to what was the status of the sod replacement. On 7/10/14, it was indicated that, *"The rain is affecting the ability to harvest the sod, and you wanted to ensure that the sod we get is top notch. That being said, it may run into early next week before you can get the sod".*

On 7/17/14, I called inquiring about the sod replacement. You indicated that you had called Super Sod on 7/16/14, but had not heard back from them. You speculated they were having some quality problem. You also indicated that you would be contacting a Manager at Super Sod.

I would appreciate you escalating this issue to the appropriate individuals at Super-Sod, in order to replace all the "dead" sod that was installed.

Sincerely,

Abbie Thornton

Letter #2

2135 Light Brigade Drive
Matthews, NC 28105
August 6, 2014

Nick Sagnella
Intrinity Landscaping
9331 Barkridge Road
Mint Hill, NC 28227

Subject: Replacement of Super-Sod's St. Augustine Sod

This memo is a follow-up to our recent conversations regarding the sod replacement.

On Thursday, July 24, 2014 you indicated via voice mail that you received my letter dated July 19, 2014. You also said that you spoke with Super Sod and they indicated they are having issues. However, they would be able to get sod shortly, since they are getting better quality. You also said you would keep me posted.

I called you on Thursday, July 31, 2014 inquiring of the status of the sod replacement. You indicated via voice mail that you talked with Brandon at Super Sod, and that "we would not be able to get the St. Augustine sod from the farm the original sod came from due to quality issues. He said he did not want to send another 'sketchy' product out from that farm".

Nevertheless, it was indicated that Super Sod is working with other sod producers in the area to obtain the St. Augustine sod. Brandon will be calling you on August 1, 2014 with an update; and that we are just waiting to get the product. I asked you to please keep me posted.

On August 1, 2014, I called you to discuss the replacement sod issue in more detail. You indicated the Super Sod farm would not be cutting any more sod this season, and that they are working with some farms not affiliated with Super Sod to obtain the St. Augustine. Super Sod was to call you on Monday, August 4, 2014 and let you know if they are able to get the sod from another supplier. Also, it was indicated that if the sod is not installed by 8/15/14, then it would be have to done next year. You mentioned that you would provide me something in writing regarding the replacement.

When I called you on Monday, August 4, 2014, you had not heard from Super Sod; so you called and left a message and text for Brandon.

I indicated that if no definite decision has been made by end of day on Tuesday, August 5, 2014; then we would need to proceed with obtain a written document from Intrinity Landscaping and Super Sod on their intentions to replace all the dead sod in my yard next year.

Today is Wednesday, August 6, 2014 and I have not received a response from you.

I have been very patient and understanding and have allowed adequate time for the sod issue to be rectified. I have initiated all of the inquiries regarding the replacement status; and this is my final communication.

I would like to go on record that I will be pursuing other measures regarding the poor quality of sod that was installed in my yard on June 28, 2014.

Sincerely,

Abbie Thornton

MEMO TO THE FILE
September 5, 2014

On September 5, 2014, I had a heated conversation with Nick Sagnella regarding the "Sod Replacement" concern. Nick indicated he made an attempt to contact me to let me know that they were in a position to replace the sod. Below is a summary of activities that took place from the time I sent Nick a letter on August 6th to September 5th.

- I sent Nick a written letter on August 6, 2014 summarizing our previous communications, and my plan to pursue other measures to address the sod replacement issue.
- It was 10 day later when Nick called me on August 16, 2014 and left a voice mail message. I have not listened to the voice mail because he had indicated to me previously that is would not be a good idea to install any sod after August 15, 2014.
- On August 15, 2014 Bank of America sent me a letter indicating they had received my dispute; and that they had requested additional information from the merchant. I suspect that the only reason he called me on August 16, 2104 was because Bank of America had contacted him regarding my dispute. Then all of sudden there is sod that is available to be installed. In the meantime, I had not received a response to my letter dated August 6, 2014.
- On August 20, 2014, Bank of America requested that I obtain a professional opinion from an individual in the sod installation business regarding the state of my yard.
- On August 22, 2014, I sent the professional opinion letter to Bank of America.
- On August 28, 2014, Bank of America notified me that my account had been credited for the $4,237.50 charge.
- On September 2, 2014, I received another voice mail from Nick, of which I have not listened to. At this time, I am sure Bank of America has notified him about the credit that was issued.
- On September 5, 2014 I called Nick. I indicated that I had asked for a letter on Intrinity and Super Sod letterhead indicating my sod would be replaced next year. Nick indicated that he is not obligated to give me any thing in writing and that it was not fair for me to dispute the charge. I indicated that since I did not hear from him when he said he would follow-up with me; and since I had not received anything from anyone in writing regarding the sod replacement; my only option was to dispute the charge for leverage.

The conversation ended with no resolution. As of today, I still have not received anything regarding replacement of the sod.

Sincerely,

Abbie Thornton

Dispute of Charges to Bank of America

2135 Light Brigade Drive
Matthews, NC 28105
November 21, 2014

Bank of America
Commercial Claims Department
P. O. Box 53101
Phoenix, AZ 85072-6413

Subject: Case ID# 8738655 (Second Dispute) Credit Card Ending – 9527

The purpose of this memo is to dispute a second charge from Intrinity Landscaping in the amount of $4,237.50, dated June 21, 2014, reference number **24431064173200748300011**.

- On November 20, 2014, I received a voice mail from Bank of America Dispute Claims Division (Tomeko Smith) indicating that they have heard from the Merchant and that I had only **one** day to contact Bank of America before my card is re-charged for the $4, 237.50 that was credited on August 28, 2014.
- I contacted Bank of America (Tomeko Smith) on November 20th , and I inquired as to why I only had one day to respond, and the Merchant was given 45 days from the date the credit was issued to me to respond. As of today, it has been approximately 80 days since the credit was issued.
    - Also during the conversation with Tomeko, it was indicated that there was no letter on file regarding a professional opinion from an individual in the area of sod installation. This professional opinion letter had been faxed to Bank of America on **August 22, 2014**; and the letter was faxed again on **August 29, 2014**. I am faxing the letter again today for the third time.
    - Tomeko indicated that the Merchant has agreed to issue me a credit of approximately $220 to cover 75 pieces of sod. This is unacceptable.
    - As I indicated to Tomeka, in my letter to Rick Sagnella on July 19th, I said that there were **over** 75 areas (not pieces) of obviously dead sod in my yard. After counting 75 areas, I just stop counting because I was so frustrated with the way my yard looked. I was under the opinion that Intrinity Landscaping would be replacing **all** the area of dead sod in my yard. For some reason, Nick Sagnella is focusing on 75 pieces of sod.

As I was making efforts to have Intrinity Landscaping to replace all the dead sod in my yard, additional sod was dying. From June 28th to August 6th, my yard went from bad to worse. As a result of Intrinity Landscaping not replacing the dead sod, I would like to dispute the full amount (another $4,237.50). Tomeko included these comments in my file.

I will have to have my entire yard re-done, which will result in me paying another $8000 or more to someone else.

On July 19th, I documented some of my observations during the sod installation. See attached "Memo to the File", along with additional pictures of the sod pallets. This memo further confirms that the quality of the sod was of poor quality. You will notice that the sod pallet have a lot of dead sod throughout. I see more dirt than "greenery".

As you will also see in the attached document, "**7 Deadly Sins of Watering New Sod and Supplemental Instructions**" on SuperSod Letterhead; SuperSod prides itself in delivering fresh cut sod of the highest quality. My expectation was that I would be receiving high quality sod. In my previous letters to Nick Sagnella on August 6th, SuperSod had indicated that they were having quality issues and they did not want to send another "sketchy" products from their farm.

Tomeko inquired as to whether I had a written contract with Intrinity Landscaping guaranteeing the quality of the sod. I indicated I did not have a written contract. However, as you are aware legal contract can be written and oral. The components of a contract include the following:
1. Offer – this includes quantity, size, color and quality
2. Acceptance – I said yes
3. Consideration – I paid $8,475 to Intrinity Landscaping
4. Capacity – I am of good mind and has the ability to understand
5. Agreement – meeting of the minds
6. Legality – it is not illegal to install sod

In essence, I paid for a high quality product that I did not receive. This would be considered a breach of contract.

Sincerely,

Abbie Thornton

Attachments (11 pages)

Metro Greenscape – Second Opinion

2135 Light Brigade Drive
Matthews, NC 28105
August 22, 2014

Commercial Dispute Department
P. O. Box 53101
Phoenix, AZ 85072

Subject: Case ID# - 8738655

Attached is the additional information requested regarding obtaining a second opinion on the SOD that was installed.

A total of 2 pages are included.

Sincerely

Abbie Thornton

METROGREENSCAPE

1622 Parker Drive
Charlotte, NC 28208

Abbie Thornton
2135 Light Brigade Drive
Matthews, NC 28105

Re: Opinion on condition of turfgrass.

Abbie,

After walking the site to observe conditions, inspecting the turfgrass and after careful consideration I offer the following as an assessment.

First some information about the type of grass in question, Mercedes St. Augustine.

Mercedes St. Augustine grass has great shade tolerance, exhibits superior heat and cold tolerance, performing well in this area.

You mentioned you had been advised that seed was present in the sod and should germinate and fill in the areas that died out but Mercedes St. Augustine turfgrass is only propagated vegetatively (meaning from cuttings rooting into soil) and is not available via seed.

You mentioned as well you had been advised that your installer was checking with other sod growers for replacement options but Mercedes St. Augustine sod is a proprietary variety of the Patten Seed Company and Super-Sod so it's only produced and distributed by Super-Sod farms.

My opinion of the condition of the existing turf and installation is the following:

1) It appears the preparation of the grade was done satisfactorily.

2) You stated the turf was laid timely upon delivery.

3) You have irrigation and it does not appear that the turf has been watered incorrectly.

4) The necrotic areas are in the shape of individual sod pieces leading me to say this is not due to insects or diseases which would not attack individual pieces.

Thus I think that some of the sod delivered was either cut too thin with not enough soil attached or it was too dry upon delivery to recover from harvesting and take root.

My suggestion to correct would be to cut out the dead areas and replace with viable sod.

Sincerely,

David Maner

Engagement Letter: 5/27/2015

THE LAW OFFICES OF T. MICHAEL TODD, P.L.L.C.
1230 WEST MOREHEAD STREET, SUITE 302
CHARLOTTE, NORTH CAROLINA 28208-5206

	TELEPHONE	
	(704) 343-9700	
		MAILING ADDRESS
T. MICHAEL TODD	FASCIMILE	POST OFFICE BOX 32422
DEBRA J. CLARK	(704) 343-0944	CHARLOTTE, NC 28232-2422

May 27, 2015

PRIVILEGED & CONFIDENTIAL

VIA ELECTRONIC MAIL
atitacs@aol.com

Ms. Abbie Thornton
2135 Light Brigade Drive
Mathews, North Carolina 28105

Dear Ms. Thornton:

We are pleased that you have decided to engage the Law Offices of T. Michael Todd, P.L.L.C. (the "Firm") to represent you in connection with a disputed service agreement and bill pertaining to landscaping work performed by Intrinity Landscaping, L.L.C. (the "Engagement").

Scope of Engagement

As described to us, the Engagement involves reviewing documents and investigating issues to pursue a defense and/or claim relating to landscaping work performed by Intrinity Landscaping, L.L.C. ("Intrinity") at your residence on or about June 28, 2014, and specifically whether or not Intrinity installed defective grass products for which you were unreasonably charged for. The services provided by the Firm in connection with the Engagement will encompass all services normally and reasonably associated with this type of engagement which the Firm is requested and able to provide and which are consistent with its professional ethical obligations.

Engagement Personnel

I will primarily be responsible for and actively involved in the Engagement. However, the work required associated with the Engagement, or parts of it, may be performed by other firm personnel, including lawyers and legal assistants. Such delegation may be for the purpose of involving other lawyers from other law firms with expertise in a given area or for the purpose of providing services on an efficient and timely basis.

Fees and Expenses

We have agreed to provide our legal services to you without charging you our customary fees for our time and expertise. As such, this matter is being handled as a *Pro Bono* matter.

Communications and Confidentiality

We have available Internet communication procedures that allow our attorneys to use e-mail for client communications in many instances. Accordingly, unless you specifically direct us otherwise in writing, we may use unencrypted e-mail sent on the Internet to communicate with you and any other entity or individual as it directly pertains to the Engagement.

We recognize our obligation to preserve the confidentiality of attorney-client communications as well as client confidences, as required by the governing rules of professional conduct. If the Engagement involves transactions, litigation, administrative proceedings or like proceedings, in which the Firm appears as counsel of record for you in publically available records, we reserve the right to inform others of the fact of our representation of you in the Engagement and the results obtained, unless you direct us otherwise in writing.

Disclaimer

The Firm has made no promises or guarantees to you about the outcome of the Engagement, and nothing in this letter shall be construed as such a promise or guarantee.

Waivers and Related Matters

The Firm represents a broad base of clients on a variety of legal matters. In some instances, the applicable rules of professional conduct may limit the Firm's ability to represent clients with conflicting or potentially conflicting interest. Those rules of professional conduct often allow the Firm to exercise its independent judgment in determining whether its relationship with one client prevents it from representing another. In other situations, the firm may be permitted to represent a client only if the other clients consent to that representation.

From time to time, the Firm may concurrently represent one client in a particular case or matter and, at the same time, our firm may be asked to represent an adversary of that same client in an unrelated case or matter. We would consider doing so *only* if it is the Firm's professional judgment that the Firm could undertake the concurrent representation impartially and without any adverse effect on the responsibilities that the Firm has to either client.

By accepting these terms, it is expressly understood and agreed that we may continue to represent, or may undertake in the future to represent, existing or new clients in any matter that is not substantially related to the Engagement, even if the interests of such clients in those other matters may be or are directly adverse to you.

Document Retention

At the close of any matter, the Firm sends its files associated with that matter to a storage facility for storage at the Firm's expense. Closed files placed into storage will remain there for six (6) years. After that time, the Firm will destroy the documents in the stored files.

At the conclusion of the Engagement, the firm will return to you any documents that are specifically requested by you to be returned. As to any documents so returned, the Firm may elect to keep a copy of the documents in our stored files.

Termination

At any time, you may, with or without cause, terminate the Engagement by notifying us of your intention to do so. During the course of the Engagement, the Firm may encounter situations that may hinder its ability to provide effective legal services to you. Should the Firm encounter a situation just described, and determine that it is not feasible or prudent to continue representation, the Firm may use its best judgment and withdraw as counsel. As such, the Firm expressly retains the right to withdraw as counsel based on its judgment.

* * *

The provisions of this letter will continue in force and effect, including if the Firm's representation of you was ended at your election (which you would be free to do at any time) or by the Firm (which would be subject to ethical requirements). In addition, the provisions of this letter will apply to future engagements of the Firm by you unless we mutually agree otherwise in writing or by a subsequent engagement letter.

This agreement shall be governed by and interpreted in accordance with the laws of the State of North Carolina without regard to conflicts of laws principles.

If the terms of this letter are satisfactory, please sign and date a copy of it and return it to me vie e-mail. If you would like to discuss any provision contained herein, please do not hesitate to contact me.

Again, we very much appreciate the opportunity to work with you and look forward to doing so.

[SIGNATURES ON PAGE IMMEDIATLEY FOLLOWING]

Sincerely,

THE LAW OFFICES OF T. MICHAEL TODD, P.L.L.C.

BY: _____
　　　T. Michael Todd

TMT/lfg

MS. ABBIE THORNTON

Dated this 27 day of _May_____, 2015.

PRINT: _Abbie Thornton_

SIGN: _Abby Thornton_

[END OF DOCUMENT]

Department of Justice Correspondences

State of North Carolina
Department of Justice
9001 Mail Service Center
Raleigh, NC 27699-9001

June 1, 2015

ROY COOPER
ATTORNEY GENERAL

CONSUMER PROTECTION
Toll Free in NC
(877) 566-7226
Outside of NC
(919) 716-6000
Fax: (919) 716-6050

Intrinity Landscaping
9331 Barkridge Road
Mint Hill, NC 28227

Re: File No. 1506194
Abbie Thornton
2135 Light Brigade Drive
Matthews, NC 28105

Dear Sir:

The Consumer Protection Division has received the attached complaint regarding your business.

In order to assess the merits of the complaint and to determine appropriate action, we need to know your position and any proposed resolution. Therefore, we ask that you provide a written statement of your position, along with copies of any supporting documents, within fifteen (15) business days of the date of this letter.

Please refer to our File Number 1506194 when you correspond with our office concerning this matter. If you prefer to submit your response electronically, we request that you do so using your business letterhead, indicating the name of the person sending the response and the sender's contact information. An electronic response should be sent to consumer@ncdoj.gov and cannot exceed 5 mb, including attachments.

Thank you for your cooperation.

Sincerely,

Maria Harkley
Consumer Protection Specialist
CONSUMER PROTECTION DIVISION

Enclosure

cc: Abbie Thornton

State of North Carolina

ROY COOPER
ATTORNEY GENERAL

Department of Justice
9001 Mail Service Center
Raleigh, NC 27699-9001

June 22, 2015

CONSUMER PROTECTION
Toll Free in NC
(877) 566-7226
Outside of NC
(919) 716-6000
Fax: (919) 716-6050

Intrinity Landscaping
9331 Barkridge Road
Mint Hill, NC 28227

Re: File No. 1506194
Abbie Thornton
2135 Light Brigade Drive
Matthews, NC 28105

Dear Sir:

Our office recently wrote to you regarding the above referenced file and requested a response within fifteen business days. To date, we have received no response. It is important that you respond to our office in writing as soon as possible as to your position on the matter. In your response, be certain to refer to File Number 1506194 and attach any supporting documents that you believe are necessary.

Actions by this office are often based on the cumulative record reflected in the complaints we receive. In addition, information about complaints filed with our office is provided in response to public inquiries. Therefore, your response is important to assure that our files accurately reflect your position regarding this matter.

If you prefer to submit your response electronically, we request that you do so using your business' letterhead, indicating the name of the person sending the response and the sender's contact information. An electronic response should be sent to consumer@ncdoj.gov and cannot exceed 5 mb, including attachments.

If you have any questions, please contact us.

Sincerely,

Maria Harkley
Consumer Protection Specialist
CONSUMER PROTECTION DIVISION

cc: Abbie Thornton

ROY COOPER
ATTORNEY GENERAL

State of North Carolina

Department of Justice
9001 Mail Service Center
Raleigh, NC 27699-9001
July 10, 2015

CONSUMER PROTECTION
Toll Free In NC
(877) 566-7226
Outside of NC
(919) 716-6000
Fax: (919) 716-6050

CERTIFIED MAIL
RETURN RECEIPT REQUESTED

Intrinity Landscaping
9331 Barkridge Road
Mint Hill, NC 28227

Re: File No. 1506194
Abbie Thornton
2135 Light Brigade Drive
Matthews, NC 28105

Dear Sir:

The Consumer Protection Division has written you twice regarding Ms. Thornton's complaint. We have yet to receive a response stating your position. As you may be aware, information about complaints filed with our office is available to the public. In addition, actions taken by the office are often based on the complaints we receive. The failure of a company to respond to complaints is a significant factor in determining whether other efforts, such as conducting a more involved investigation, are appropriate.

Please respond to this office immediately as to the disposition of this matter, including in your response a reference to File Number 1506194. If you prefer to submit your response electronically, we request that you do so using your business's letterhead, indicating the name of the person sending the response and the sender's contact information. An electronic response should be sent to consumer@ncdoj.gov and cannot exceed 5 mb, including attachments.

Sincerely,

Maria Harkley
Consumer Protection Specialist
CONSUMER PROTECTION DIVISION

cc: Abbie Thornton
Intrinity Landscaping/Concord

Counter Suit Documentation – Court Date

The following information was used to defend myself during the court case on 11/20/2015.

Chronology of Sod Installations at 2135 Light Brigade Drive, Matthews, NC 28105

Exhibit A: Proposal and Acceptance from Intrinity Landscape to install 9450 Sq. Ft. of Mercedes St. Augustine sod in the amount of $8,475.00.

Exhibit B: Credit card receipts of payment made in the amount of $4,237.50 on June 21, 2014 and June 28, 2014.

Exhibit C: Pictures of sod condition upon delivery on June 27, 2014.

Exhibit D: July 19, 2014 letter sent to Intrinity Landscape concerning replacement of dead sod. I notified Intrinity Landscape of the dead sod on July 2, 2014, which was nine (9) days after the initial installation.

Exhibit E: July 19, 2014 "memo to the file" documenting my observations while the sod was being installed. Nick delivered another pallet of sod; and the installers took the dead pieces of sod from back yard after they ran out of sod.

Exhibit F: August 6, 2014 letter to Intrinity Landscape inquiring about the status of SuperSOD finding sod from another supplier because they were having quality issues at their sod farm and would not be cutting any more sod this season. It was also indicated that if the sod was not installed by August 15, 2014, then it would need to be done in 2015. I requested that SuperSod and Intrinity Landscape providing me a letter in writing indicating that they would replace my sod in 2015.

Exhibit G: August 6, 2014. I disputed the second credit card payment made to Intrinity Landscape. I was asked to obtain a professional opinion letter by Bank of America. It was later indicated by Bank of America that they did not received the professional opinion letter. This letter was faxed to Bank of America three (3) times. Intrinity Landscape agreed to accept responsibility for only $203.40 As a result, on 12/16/2014, Bank of America reversed the charge of $4,034.10 back to my account.

Exhibit H: August 6, 2014 pictures of my yard on the date the dispute was sent to Bank of America.

Exhibit I: August 22, 2014 Professional Opinion Letter from MetroGreenscape on the condition of the Turfgrass.

Exhibit J: September 5, 2014 Memo to the file after having a heated discussion with Nick Sagnella regarding the sod replacement. Nick only contacted me after he was notified by Bank of America that I had disputed a charge.

Exhibit K: November 21, 2014. Disputed the first credit card payment made to Intrinity Landscape. At this time, I sent the document with a "returned receipt" through the mail, as well as faxed the documents, and stayed on the phone with a representative at Bank Of America confirming they received the fax. On November 26, 2014, Bank of America issued me a credit back to my account for the $4,237.50.

Exhibit L: St. Augustine Maintenance Schedule, Credit card receipts of purchased products to maintain yard. SuperSod's Supplemental Instruction where they have indicated that; *"You have purchased a top quality turf grass that is the result of more than 50 years of experience."* On 4/27/2015, I seeked Legal Counsel and discontinued any maintenance on the grass due to it being "DEAD"

Exhibit M: April 27, 2015 pictures of the condition of the sod in my yard that Intrinity Landscape installed.

Exhibit N: April 27, 2015 picture of the condition of sod that I had to install on the right side of my house that was left undone by Intrinity; and the related 2014 and 2015 credit card receipts of products that I purchased to install sod.

Exhibit O: May 6, 2015. Filed a complaint against the BBB. Since he was not BBB accredited, they could not assist me.

Exhibit P: June 22, 2015. A complaint was filed with the Department of Justice. Intrinity Landscape responded August 4, 2105 with a response. His response was implying that I had been out of town several weeks at a time, and my yard was not being maintained and that was the reason my yard was in the condition that it was. As an FYI, I would fly out of town on Monday morning and back either Thursday or Friday. See maintenance program in **Exhibit L**.

Exhibit Q: June 1, 2015 Proposal and Acceptance with Secure Turf Inc. to removed dead sod and to install 6559 sq. ft. of sod in the amount of $10, 535.55. Loan in the amount of $10,000 financed through EnerBankUSA to pay Secure Turf for dead sod removal and installation of new sod.

Exhibit R: June 24, 2015 Payment Authorization form for EnerBankUSA to pay SecureTurf $10,000. Note that I financed the loan to pay Secure Turf through EnerBankUSA.

> Note: Secure Turf ordered 6559 sq. ft. of sod and it covered the same area that I had paid Intrinity Landscape to cover with 9450 sq. ft. (difference of 2891 sq. ft.). This further confirms my suspicion that Intrinity Landscape did not purchase the sod I paid for, and probably had an agreement with a friend to off-load low quality sod to clients and keep the money. I paid for 9450sq. ft of Sod that did not cover the area prepared for the installation.

Exhibit S: July 12, 2015 pictures of my yard re-done by Secure Turf on June 24, 2015

Exhibit T: A 4.29 minutes video of yard taken on 7/10/2014 on my iPhone.

Exhibit U: A 6.31 minutes vide of yard taken on 9/12/2014 on my iPhone

Note: The countersuit should be in the amount of $4, 034.10.

Judgement

The Judge granted the judgement for me in the amount of $3,237.00.

[Court judgment form - rotated sideways on page - STATE OF NORTH CAROLINA, Mecklenburg County, In the General Court Of Justice, District Court Division-Small Claims. File No. 15 CVM 13170. JUDGMENT IN ACTION TO RECOVER MONEY OR PERSONAL PROPERTY. Plaintiff: Intrinity Landscaping LLC, 1446 Biltmore Drive, Concord, NC 28205. Versus Defendant: Abbie Thorton, 2135 Light Brigade Drive, Matthews, NC. Principal Sum Of Judgment: $3,237.00. Total Amount: $3,237.00. Plaintiff awarded $3,237.00 pursuant to counter-claim (breach of contract). Signed 11/20/15.]

Mutual Dismissal With Prejudice

Intrinity subsequently decided to challenge the judgement by obtaining legal counsel. His lawyer informed him that it would cost him more to go to court than he would if the case was dismissed. On December 10, 2015, the case was dismissed with prejudice. See below:

STATE OF NORTH CAROLINA	IN THE GENERAL COURT OF JUSTICE
MECKLENBURG COUNTY	DISTRICT COURT DIVISION
	~~14-CVM-13120~~

INTRINITY LANDSCAPING, LLC,

   Plaintiff,

v.

ABBIE THORNTON,

   Defendant.

MUTUAL DISMISSAL WITH PREJUDICE

Pursuant to Rule 41 of the North Carolina Rules of Civil Procedure, Plaintiff Intrinity Landscaping, LLC and Defendant Abbie Thornton mutually dismiss all claims asserted against one another in this lawsuit, with prejudice.

This the 10 day of Dec, 2015.

_____
Harrison A. Lord
State Bar No. 36236
5821 Fairview Rd
Suite 100
Charlotte, North Carolina 28209
hal@bernhardtlaw.net
704-335-0444 (phone)
704-335-0551 (fax)
Attorneys for Plaintiff

_____
T. Michael Todd
State Bar No. 8069
1230 W. Morehead Street, Suite 302
Charlotte, N.C. 28208
tmtodd@aol.com
704-343-9700
Attorney for Defendant

PART V

TRANSPORTATION

LETTER 16: Moving from Philly
(Stevens Relocation) - September 12, 2014

I had been working in Philadelphia, Pennsylvania on a contract job for approximately 2 years. I had gotten an apartment because it was cheaper than staying in a hotel. It was mentioned to me that the contract was not going to be renewed, so I should not plan to be working on the contract after the current one expires. Subsequently, the contract was renewed but I decided to move anyway.

During August 2014, I made plans to have my furniture moved to Raleigh, North Carolina to my daughter's house. I contacted several moving companies to obtain quotes. The Salesperson at Stevens Relocation had gone beyond the call of duty to convince me that the quote he was providing was the most economical and efficient. He quoted approximately $1000 for the move based on the items I had indicated I wanted them to move. These items included a king size bedroom suite, a couch, loveseat, and two end tables and a coffee table. So, I decided to go with Stevens Relocation.

Once the movers arrived and loaded the truck, the actual cost was twice as much as what was quoted. I had to either decide to have them unpack the truck or pay the amount. I attempted to have several conversations with Stevens Relocation prior to deciding to move forward but could never speak with the right person at the time. I felt stuck between a rock and a hard place at the time. I decided to pay the amount since my daughter had made plans for the delivery in her home.

I wrote the following letter to the General Manager of Stevens Relocation asking for a refund of the amount I had paid over the original quote, but I never did get a response.

2135 Light Brigade Drive
Matthews, NC 28105
September 12, 2014

Anthony Demarco, General Manager
Stevens Relocation
2626 East 14 Street
Brooklyn, NY 11235

Subject: Request for refund – B2392434

I would like to request a refund in the amount of **$1,225.00** related to moving estimate #B2392434.

- On August 6, 2014, John Galler, Salesperson provided me an estimate on my move to North Carolina. At this time, I provided John Galler with the specific items I wanted move. These items are noted in the enclosed email dated August 6, 2014. (see enclosure)
- Based on the information I provided, John Galler quoted me an estimate of $1000. He also indicated that Stevens have trucks going to North Carolina several times a week, and that the delivery could be made within 1-4 days. We agreed to a move date of September 11, 2014. (see enclosure)
- On September 8, 2014, I called your Company to confirm that the move was still schedule for September 11, 2014. At this time, I was informed that John Galler was no longer with your company. The person I spoke with indicated she was reviewing all of John Galler's sales, because it appeared, he was less than honest in dealing with potential customers. She indicated the delivery would be between 7-10 days.
- On September 11, 2014 the movers arrived at my apartment. At this time, Johnnie indicated the items I wanted moved was much more than 200 cubic feet.
- We call the office and spoke with Patricia regarding my concern. She indicated that maybe I may have to pay a few more hundred dollars over the $1000. So, I agreed to proceed with the move.
- After the truck was loaded, Johnnie called your office and indicated my furniture took approximately 500 cubit feet instead, resulting in an additional $1500.
- I am currently outraged that your Company would allow their sales people to partake in such deceptive practices. It was very obvious that the quote that was provided by John Galler was purposely misleading to obtain my business.

After your company realized John Galler were involved in these deceptive practices and was subsequently fired; no one reviewed my estimated and contacted me as to whether what was quoted was reasonable. It is highly unlikely that anyone could be that far off when I itemized what I specifically wanted move.

After the truck was loaded by the movers, I had to make a decision as to whether they should unload the truck and put my furniture back into my apartment; or pay the full amount. I decided to pay the amount ($2,225) so the movers could leave my apartment, and I had a plane to catch.

I spoke with Joseph Russo, Operations Manager regarding the situation, and he indicated that he could only grant me a $175 administrative discount. This is unacceptable.

I called and left a voice mail for you on September 11, 2014 but have not heard from you so far. I would appreciate you making this right.

Sincerely,

Abbie Thornton

Enclosures

Where are They Now

Today is May 12, 2020. I decided to search the internet to see what the status of the Stevens Relocation company.

They currently have a one star rating, and when trying to log onto their website (www.stevenrelocation.com) , the site could not be found.

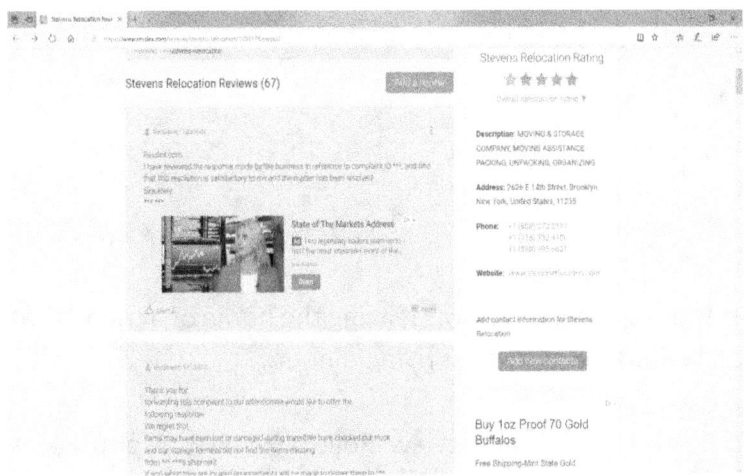

Response when logging on to website
(www.stevensrelocation.com)

I am concluding the company is no longer in business based on the above search. It appears that their deceptive practices caught up with them.

LETTER 17: Potholes Blow-out on Thanksgiving Day

(NC Department of Transportation) - November 22, 2018

On Thanksgiving Day, I was leaving the home of a friend that had invited me to Thanksgiving dinner.

While traveling on Lakeview Road around 5:15pm, I was headed towards W. T. Harris Blvd in Charlotte, North Carolina and my car dropped into a huge "hole" in the road. I did not realize until approximately a mile later that my right front and rear wheels and rims had been damaged.

The Department of Transportation was working on the road at the time and did not have the holes covered up or adequate re-routing of the traffic or signage to prevent the drop into the hole.

I started to hear this loud sound and found out that my front tire had gone flat, so I pulled off the road and called a friend for help. It was dark and I could not see, nor did I have a flashlight. When he inspected the tire, he indicated that both the right front and rear tires had been damaged as well as the rims. He was able to use my spare for the front right wheel and he followed me home for safety.

The next day, which was Friday, November 23, 2018, I went to Discount Tire on Albemarle Road in Charlotte to have them inspect the tires and rims. They indicated that I needed to have the rims and tires replaced because they were not repairable. Also, since I had the original rims on my 1987 Volvo 740, they were not able to locate those rims. I had to purchase a new set of 4 rims and 4 tires. This amounted to **$827.81**. See the picture of the new rims and the receipt for the purchase of them below:

New Tires and Rims

Discount Tire Receipt

DISCOUNT TIRE 11/23/2018 2:57 PM

ABBIE THORNTON
2135 LIGHT BRIGADE DRIVE
MATTHEWS, NC 28105
704.622.6982 (M)

1987 VOLVO Plate#: HEAVENS
740 Miles: 660,125
TR GUGLE Torque Spec: 65

NCC 98 Invoice #
9315 ALBEMARLE RD 445691B
CHARLOTTE, NC 28227
704.536.2996

Salesperson 55
IRWIN M GARCIA

Article	Qty	Description	FET	Price	Amount
55411	4	P 185 /60 R15 88H SL RSW SNT SENTURY TOURING TIRE MILEAGE WARRANTY 60000 ROTATION P 30 R 30 BOLT PATTERN 5 - 100	42.00		168.30
88017	4	CERTIFICATES FOR REFUND, REPLACEMENT For the certificate details, see www.discounttire.com/customer--service/certificates		9.50	37.00
80675	4	STATE REQUIRED ENVIRONMENTAL FEE		.84	3.36
99224	4	WASTE TIRE DISPOSAL FEE		1.75	7.00
88219	4	INSTALLATION & LIFE OF TIRE MAINTENANCE Terms and Conditions can be found at www.discounttire.com/customer--service/invoice--terms		20.00	20.00
67192	1	MULTI - LEVEL TE ONLINE/MAIL - IN 11/22/18			

TEST FIT

77986	4	18 X7 5 - 100 OS/118.30 ZV BLMCM5 VW SDA 70.16		109.00	436.00
		WARRANTY -- w structural 1 year finish			
47940	1	8100 .60 SD 1 4" GL ZN SL HDWARE LUG LUG KIT BTN29A		46.00	46.00
11382	-1	185 /70 R14 88T SL RSW BAR BARUM BRILLANTIS 2		36.00	-36.00
11387	1	185 /70 R14 88T SL RSW BAR BARUM BRILLANTIS 2 TIRE MILEAGE WARRANTY 60000 ROTATION F 30 R 30		38.00	38.00
80617	6	CERTIFICATES FOR REFUND, REPLACEMENT		7.00	
80675	1	STATE REQUIRED ENVIRONMENTAL FEE		.79	.79
67192	1	MULTI - LEVEL REBATE ONLINE/MAIL - IN 11/22/18 - 11/28/18			

COMMENT 11-22-2018 2:39 PM

The tire and/or wheel you have chosen is different
from the original equipment provided with your
vehicle and may change its handling or stability
characteristics
Further information able from you
Disc n a

I u y signature below: The personal
i mation I have voluntarily
rect. I agree to purchase the
y the fees, and authorize the service
rs at the final costs specifically listed
o electronic invoice. This invoice, if and
an necessary under the law, is as estimate of
repair and service costs as olled herein. Term
and Conditions by this tr etion are found at
www.discounttire.com/c uuer--service/invoice--terms

Sub Total: 772.12
Sales Tax: 55.69
Sales Total: 827.81

LGXXX3XXX140 End Charge Tendered 827.81 (VISA)
Tendered Today 827.81

Tendered Total 827.81

Signature on file

NCDOT Citizen Incident Statement

On January 19, 2019 I then completed and mailed *"Form 141, North Carolina Department of Transportation Citizen Incident Statement"* with the information mentioned above. Additionally, I sent them pictures of the damaged tires and rims as well as the receipt from Discount Tires showing where I had to purchase a new set of rims and tires for $827.81.

Form 141 (pages 1-3)

Form 141
Rev 12/1/2005

North Carolina Department of Transportation
Citizen Incident Statement

This form is designed to assist in reporting an incident resulting in damage or injury that involved the North Carolina Department of Transportation.

GENERAL INFORMATION:
(Please fill out General Information for either vehicle incident or property incident)

1. Your Name: Abbie Thornton
2. Your Address: 10555 Parkhouse Lane
   City: Charlotte State: NC Zip Code: 28269
3. Telephone: Business: (704) 622-6982 Home: (   )
4. Date of Incident: 11/22/2018 Time: 5:15 pm Location: Lakeview Road

5. State Agency Involved in Incident: NC Dept of Transportation
6. State employee you consider responsible for the Incident:
7. Address:
8. Explain in your own words how you were injured or damaged and in what way you believe the State employee was responsible.

While traveling on Lakeview Road, heading towards West W T Harris Blvd, my car dipped into a huge "hole" in the road causing the right front and rear wheels and rims to be damaged.

Prior to reaching West W.T. Harris, the tires were flat and I had to pull off the road and call for assistance.

I believe the DOT is responsible because there were no obvious signs of road construction, and the huge hole had not been covered.

Form 141
Rev 12/1/2005

INCIDENT INVOLVING A MOTOR VEHICLE: (Please fill out only if incident involved a motor vehicle)

9. Private Vehicle Involved in Incident:

Make: __Volvo__ Model: __740__ Year: __1987__

License Number: __5673186__ State: __North Carolina__

Driver: __Abbie Thornton__ Age: __59__

Owner of Vehicle: __Abbie Thornton__

Insurance Company and Policy Number: __GEICO, 4568-70-11-65__

Speed of Vehicle at the time of the incident: __20 mph__

Has the vehicle been repaired? __Yes__

If the vehicle has been repaired, state place where it was repaired: __Discount Tire, 9315 Albemarle Rd, Charlotte, NC 28227__

Cost of Repair: __$827.81__ Have the Repairs been paid for? __Yes__

If the repairs were paid for, who paid for them? __Abbie Thornton__

10. The damages consist of the following: __Two tires and rims were damaged. (Attached are photos of damage)__

11. State Vehicle:

Agency: _____ Operator: _____

Address: _____ Make of Vehicle: _____

Model: _____ Year: _____

License No.: _____ Speed of Vehicle: _____

If State Vehicle, was it a truck, state: Was it loaded _____ with what _____

How high was it loaded? _____ Was it covered? _____

12. Injuries:

Name: _____ Address: _____

Name: _____ Address: _____

Name: _____ Address: _____

Name: _____ Address: _____

13. Nature of Injuries: _____

Form 141
Rev 12/1/2005
INCIDENT INVOLVING PROPERTY DAMAGE:
(Please fill out only if incident involved property damage other than a vehicle)

18. Property Involved in Incident:

    Address: _____

    City: _____ State: _____ Zip Code: _____

19. Date of Incident: _____ Time: _____

20. State Agency Involved: _____

21. State Employee you consider responsible for the incident:
    _____

22. Address of State Employee: _____

23. State Project Number: _____

24. Contractor: _____

Provide any additional comments or attach pictures related to the incident.

Date of Report: January 19, 2019   Signature: _____

Pictures of Damage to Vehicle Tires and Rims

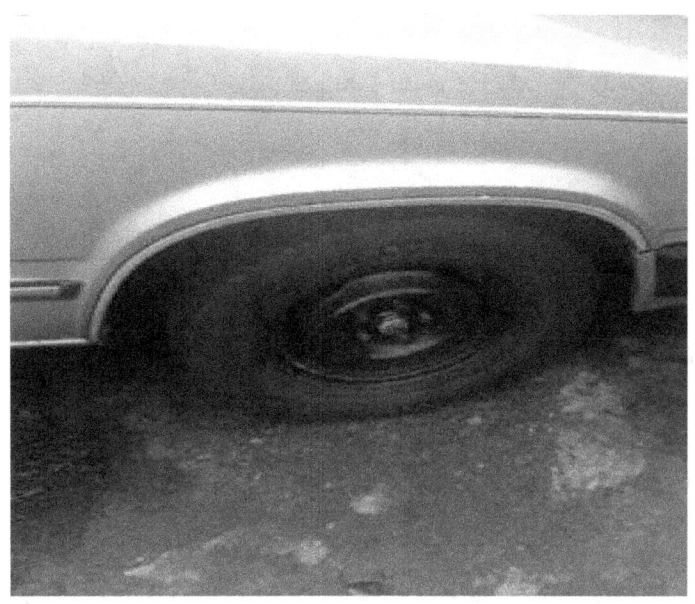

On March 9, 2019, I received a letter from the Department of Justice Attorney General office indicating that I had to prove facts and establish negligence on the part of a specific state employee. It was concluded that there was no negligence on the part of any state employee, and that I needed to file with the NC Industrial Commission, and a fee would be charged to file a claim with them.

Claim Denied
My claim was denied in letter below:

JOSHUA H. STEIN
ATTORNEY GENERAL

REPLY TO:
Crawford, David
Direct 910-397-1503
Email: DCRAWFOR@NCDOJ.GOV
FAX: 910.790.7669

March 9, 2019

Abbie Thornton
10555 Parkhouse Lane
Charlotte, NC 28269

Re: Abbie Thornton v. NC DOT
Date of Accident: November 22, 2018
Our File #: TC-19-00839

Dear Ms. Thornton:

This will acknowledge your claim for damages to your vehicle.

In order to collect from any state agency, the North Carolina Tort Claims Act requires that you prove facts that establish negligence on the part of a specific state employee. The acts of negligence must be described in detail and there must be no contributory negligence on the part of the person making the claim.

It is our position that there was no negligence on the part of any state employee and no legal liability. We regret that we are unable to consider payment of your claim.

If you feel we are incorrect, you may file a claim with the NC Industrial Commission at 1236 Mail Service Center, Raleigh, NC 27699-1326. Telephone: 919-807-2504; Fax: 919-715-0282; Web Address: http://www.ic.nc.gov. There is a filing fee which you must submit with the completed document; therefore we recommend that you inquire of the Industrial Commission as to their current fees and any additional requirements that may apply to your claim.

Very truly yours,

David Crawford

cc: Robert L. Barrier, P.E.
Jon C. Hinson, E.L, SCME

WWW.NCDOJ.GOV   114 W. EDENTON STREET, RALEIGH, NC 27603   919.716.6400
P. O. BOX 629, RALEIGH, NC 27602-0629

Response to Department of Justice Attorney General

After reading this letter and on March 13, 2019, I responded back to the Department of Justice Attorney General office indicating my disappointment and the conclusion that was drawn by their office with no inquiry or follow-up on their part. Additionally, I inquired as to why their office did not forward the information to the NC Industrial Commission and asked that they forward it. I had sent them the documentation along with the pictures of the damage. See letter below:

10555 Parkhouse Land
Charlotte, NC 28269
March 13, 2019

Mr. David Crawford
NC Dept of Justice
114 W. Edenton Street
Raleigh, NC 27603

Subject: File #: TC-19-00839

It is unfortunate that a citizen has to specifically identify a person that may have contributed to negligence as it relates to "huge cradles" and "pot-holes" in streets and roads that are left unaddressed by the Department of Transportation.

I am not privy to who is working on a particular road on any particular day and time. Additionally, I was not a supervisor on-site monitoring the actions of the employees/contractor that the Department of Transportation had working on the road. If I was able to identify a particular person, the incident would not have happened.

It should be the responsibility of the Department of Transportation and its contractors to ensure there is proper caution signage when roads are under construction and there are serious risks to drivers and vehicle, (e.g., cradles, potholes).

I have already provided all the documentation indicating that the damage happened, due to the negligence of whomever the Department of Transportation had working on that particular road during November 2018.

I do not think I should have to file another claim and incur additional costs with another NC agency. I disagree with your assessment and would appreciate you reconsidering payment of my claim. Or you can forward the information I have provided to you to the NC Industrial Commission.

Sincerely,

Abbie Thornton

On March 21, 2019, I received this hand-written note from David Crawford of the Department of Justice Attorney General office which appeared to be heated.

Josh Stein
Attorney General

3/21/19

Ms. Abbie Thornton:
19-00839

Ms. Thornton: You need to file the appeal with the NCIC. NCDOT has advised us they do not wish to pay your claim.

Enclosures
① Letter dated 3/13/19
② Denial Letter.

I am growing very tired of the government and did not pursue this any further. I have waisted so much of my time trying to get justice.

Measuring the NC DOT Performance and Accountablity

Here is the NC DOT Performance Scorecard for the 2019-20. Customer satisfaction is at a record low of 58%.

PART VI
INSURANCE COMPANIES

LETTER 18: Increase in Allstate Premiums (CitiMortgage Homeowner's Insurance) - November 18, 2016

Allstate was the homeowner's insurance company that was providing my coverage during the period November 5, 2015 to November 5, 2016. When it was time to renew my policy, I opted to cancel and not renew the policy which expired November 5, 2016. I had been using Allstate for a few years and the premium kept going up each year.

In the meantime, I elected to obtain Liberty Mutual to provide coverage for my home at 2135 Light Brigade Drive which was effective November 1, 2016.

On November 11, 2016, CitiMortgage sent me a letter indicating that they had paid the premium on my homeowner's policy to two separate insurance companies (Allstate and Liberty Mutual) within a 12-month period. They requested that I ask for a refund and send the refund check to CitiMortgage.

After reviewing my monthly mortgage statements from October 2015 to November 2016, I noted that the last payment CitiMortgage made to an insurance company for my homeowner's insurance was 10/17/2015. I asked that they provide me documentation showing where they had made a payment to the two insurance companies within the last 12 months. See letter dated November 18, 2016 below:

2135 Light Brigade Drive
Matthews, NC 28105
November 18, 2016

CitiMortgage, Inc.
P. O. Box 7706
Springfield, OH 45501

Subject: Homeowner's Insurance Coverage

This letter is in response to your letter dated November 11, 2016 regarding making payments to two different insurance companies within the last 12 months, (see attachment 1).

According to my records, the last escrow disbursement for hazard insurance was October 17, 2015, (see attachment 2).

Secondly, my insurance with Allstate (policy number 968 515 836) was not renewed, and was canceled as of November 5, 2016, (see attachment 3).

Since the effective date of the insurance with Liberty Mutual was as of November 1, 2016, I wanted to ensure that there was no lapse of coverage between the two companies.

If you have made payment to Allstate during the month of October 2016 to coverage another year, please let me know and provide me whatever correspondence indicating you have made a recent payment so that I can request a refund.

Sincerely,

Abbie Thornton

Attachments

Attachment 1

CitiMortgage

November 11, 2016

ABBIE THORNTON
2135 LIGHT BRIGADE DR
MATTHEWS NC 28105

Re: Property Address: 2135 Light Brigade Dr
Matthews NC 28105

Dear Abbie Thornton:

CitiMortgage, Inc. has recently received and paid a premium billing notice for homeowner's insurance coverage from LIBERTY MUTUAL INSURANCE with a policy effective date of November 1, 2016. Our records indicate that we have disbursed escrow funds for the payment of homeowner's insurance on the above-referenced property to two different insurance companies within the past 12 months.

If you have not already contacted your insurance company to request cancellation of your previous policy, please do so as soon as possible to prevent duplicate coverage on your property. We are not able to assist you with this action, as the mortgagee clause endorsement on the policy does not allow CitiMortgage, Inc. to cancel the coverage on your behalf.

Upon receipt of the refund check from the cancelled policy, please forward the properly endorsed check to CitiMortgage, Inc. at the address provided below. To ensure prompt processing, please include your CitiMortgage account number on the check.

> CitiMortgage, Inc.
> P. O. Box 7706
> Springfield OH 45501

Once we have received the refund check, we will deposit the funds into your escrow account to reduce the possibility of an escrow shortage related to this transaction. If the refund check is not received in our office prior to your loan's next scheduled escrow analysis, your payment may increase accordingly.

If you need further assistance regarding the property insurance for this mortgage account, please contact our Insurance Department directly at 1-800-442-8774. Our Insurance Associates are available at this number Monday through Friday from 8:00 a.m. to 10:00 p.m. and Saturday from 9:00 a.m. to 6:00 p.m., ET. TTY Services are also available. To access: Dial 711 from the United States or Dial 1-866-280-2050 from Puerto Rico. When you contact us, please refer to mortgage account number 1122934195.

Sincerely,

Insurance Department
Customer Service
CMIOPF9
TZ9

© 2016 CitiMortgage, Inc. CitiMortgage, Inc. is an equal housing lender. Citi, Arc Design, and Citi and Arc Design are registered service marks of Citigroup Inc. *Calls are randomly monitored and recorded to ensure quality service. The purpose of this communication is an attempt to collect a debt and any information obtained will be used for that purpose.

Attachment 2

Mortgage Account Information

Page 1

Statement Date: 11/11/15

Account Number: 1122934195-0
Payment Due Date: 12/01/15
Amount Due: **$2,640.76**
$88.56 late fee will be charged after 12/16/15.

How to reach us
www.citimortgage.com
Customer Service: 1-800-283-7918*
Please reference your account number 1122934195 when calling.
Calls are randomly monitored and recorded to ensure quality service.

Explanation of Amount Due

Principal	$1,831.59
Interest	$382.55
Escrow	$426.62
Total Amount Due	**$2,640.76**

Account Information

ABBIE THORNTON
Property Address: 2135 LIGHT BRIGADE DR
MATTHEWS, NC 28105

Type of Mortgage	FIXED RATE LOAN
Outstanding Principal Balance	$153,019.09
Interest Rate	3.00000%
Escrow Balance	$573.93
CitiMortgage Taxes Paid Year to Date	$4,067.73

Past Payments Breakdown

	Paid Since Last Statement	Paid Year to Date
Principal	$1,838.62	$19,859.85
Interest	$387.14	$4,507.31
Escrow	$566.14	$4,776.54
Total	**$2,791.90**	**$29,143.70**

Transaction Activity Since Last Statement (10/13/15 to 11/11/15)

Date	Description	Charges/Adjustments	Payments
10/14/15	Additional Escrow Received - Thank you		$139.52
10/17/15	Escrow Disbursement - Hazard Insurance		-$1,331.00
11/11/15	Payment Amount Received - Thank you		$2,640.76
11/11/15	Additional Principal Received - Thank you		$11.62

Important Messages

Due to year-end processing, payments received between 10 p.m. and Midnight ET on December 31st will be credited to 2015 for tax reporting purposes and posted to your account history in January 2016.

Important messages continued on the next page

To ensure timely processing, please enclose your check and the coupon below in the envelope provided.

Attachment 3

Allstate Insurance Company
Attn: MSW21 NC CTR
8711 Freeport Pkwy
Irving TX 75063

CW000#01

ABBIE THORNTON
2135 LIGHT BRIGADE DR
MATTHEWS NC 28105-6413

Information as of September 30, 2016

Policyholder(s)   Page 1 of 2
ABBIE THORNTON

Policy number
968 515 836

Policy type
Homeowners

Non-renewal date and time:
11/05/2016 at 12:01 am Standard time
At the location of the property

Your policy provided by
Allstate Indemnity Company

Your Allstate agency is
CC PARKER AGENCY
(704) 243-0404
CHARLESPARKER@ALLSTATE.COM

NOTICE OF NON-RENEWAL

Location of Property: 2135 LIGHT BRIGADE DR MATTHEWS, NC 28105-6413

We are writing to inform you that we will be unable to renew the Allstate policy identified above. Your policy will terminate as of the non-renewal date and time shown above due to the following reason(s):

We did not receive a signed Consent to Rate form from you. *If you already submitted this form or believe this mailing was sent to you in error, please contact your Allstate representative.*

As you may be aware, homeowner's insurance coverages in North Carolina are either provided at manual rates established by the North Carolina Rate Bureau or they are provided at rates determined by your insurance company. The premiums offered to you for this policy are based on rates that are higher than the North Carolina Rate Bureau's manual rates. The Consent to Rate form serves as an application for Allstate Indemnity Company, acknowledging that you accept our policy and rates. Because we did not receive this form from you, we are not able to renew your policy.

The protection provided by your policy will remain in effect until the non-renewal date and time shown above. However, in the event that any policy premiums are not paid when due, we may cancel the policy prior to that non-renewal date and time.

There was no additional correspondence received from CitiMortgage regarding paying two companies within a 12-month period, after sending the above letter to CitiMortgage.

Effective November 1, 2017, the Nationstar Mortgage LLC d/b/a Mr. Cooper started to service my mortgage loan instead of CitiMortgage.

LETTER 19: Insurance Cancellations
(Farm Bureau, Zurick, BCBS, State Farm, IBC, Allstate, Liberty Mutual) - 1990 to 2020

I.   Farm Bureau Mutual Insurance Company

I bought my first car in 1981 and it was a Mazda GLC. Farm Bureau was my insurance company, and I was living in Alabama at the time. I later moved to North Carolina during the year 1981. North Carolina had a law where everyone that was of age in your house had to be added to your automobile insurance, even though they did not have a license or was a driver of the insured's vehicle. The state assumed that if a person were of driving age, they would and could drive your vehicle. So, in 1990 Farm Bureau automatically added my daughter to my insurance policy and billed me the related rates of a 16 year old on my policy.

At this time, I canceled my insurance with Farm Bureau and went to State Farm. The members that stayed in my home was no one's business as far as I was concerned. In 1991 I moved to Ohio and kept my State Farm insurance.

II.   Zurick Medallion Financial and Insurance Services

In 2003 I started my own company, TITACS Inc. and Zurick Medallion was the company I selected to provide Errors and Omission Insurance for my company. As the years went by, I noticed that the number of "exclusions" were increasing every year as my policy was being renewed. One day, I decided to take the time to read my declaration page and my policy in full to see what coverage I had.

As it turned out, I was not being covered for what I had initially obtained the coverage for. At this point, I wrote the following letter to cancel my policy.

2135 Light Brigade Drive
Matthews, NC 28105
March 1, 2010

Joe Minervini
Medallion Insurance Services, LLC
P. O. Box 976
Waxhaw, NC 28173

Subject: Policy Cancellation – PAS 00653107

Please cancel policy effective immediately. It appears that the policy no longer covers professional liability regarding the basic premise of my Company, and specifically mentions the following exclusions:

- Electronic Data Processing Computer Consulting or Programming Prof Exclusion
- Testing or Consulting Errors and Omissions Exclusion
- Financial Services Exclusion

Sincerely,

Abbie Thornton
TITACS Inc.

A few years later, I received a letter regarding a suit related to some improprieties of Zurick Medallion Insurance Services that resulted in a refund of prior premiums.

III. BlueCross BlueShield of North Carolina (BCBSNC)

As a self employed individual, I obtained insurance through BCBS for a few years. The rate was over $300 a month at the time, and continued to go up each subsequent year.

After starting to work at Carolina Healthcare System as a full-time employee January 2011, I canceled my medical insurance with BCBSNC. See letter below:

2135 Light Brigade Drive
Matthews, NC 238105
February 25, 2011

BCBSNC
Customer Service
P. O. Box 2291
Durham, NC 27702-2291

Subject: Termination of Coverage

I would like to terminate my coverage effective March 1, 2011. My account number is **300118140**.

Sincerely,

Abbie Thornton

IV.   State Farm Insurance

When I started working for Carolina Healthcare System in January 2011, employees could use Metropolitan Insurance for their car insurance at a reduced rate. At some point during 2012, as I was backing out of my garage, I pulled the left front side fender off my BMW because I was too close to a work stand in my garage. I reported the claim to State Farm which was approximately $3500 of damage.

When my auto policy was renewed, it went up by $500 for the year. I had never had an accident during the time I was covered by State Farm from 1990 to 2012. I called my insurance agent who was based in Greensboro, NC at the time regarding the increase. His attitude was that "this is just the way it is". There was no mention of any kind of adjustment due to me being accident free for over 20 years.

On that day, I canceled my auto insurance with State Farm and went to Metropolitan Insurance through Carolina Healthcare System. When I left Carolina Healthcare System in February 2013, I was no longer eligible for insurance through Metropolitan Insurance at the reduced rate. Their regular rates were extremely high in comparison. So once the policy expired, I obtained a policy with Allstate. Allstate had a new policy deal that was comparable to the reduced rate I was receiving at Metropolitan Insurance.

Of course, all the insurance companies have these new customers one-year policy deals to entice you to go with their company. Once the one year has expired, they go to their regular rate, which are usually much higher.   After the first year with Allstate, I was looking to see what other insurance company had a new customer deal.

I was contacted by someone at State Farm concerning a new policy. After talking to the agent and receiving the quote, I decided to go back with State Farm. When I received my first bill, the amount I was billed for was not the amount I had been quoted by the agent. I called the agent to clarify the quote for the coverage, and he indicated that they thought they could provide me homeowner coverage, but could not due to me having a claim on my homeowner's insurance during 2011 for roof damage due to a hailstorm, wind and rain. This is the reason for the increases from the quoted amount. I immediately canceled the coverage. See correspondence below:

2135 Light Brigade Drive
Matthews, NC 28105
November 26, 2013

State Farm Mutual Automobile Ins. Company
1500 State Farm Blvd.
Charlottesville, VA 22909

Subject: Policy Cancellation – 165 6300-E02-33 (follow-up)

This letter is a follow-up to my original request to cancel the above policy on November 12, 2013.

I received a check in the amount of **$281.24**, which is less than the amount of the premiums paid.

I requested cancellation of the policy due to the following reasons:
1. I was mis-lead regarding the fact that State Farm would also provide homeowners' coverage.
2. The premiums quoted (**$371.88**) for the auto insurance was less than the amount (**$568.65**) that was subsequently billed.

I would appreciate you submitting the remainder of the refund that is due for the premiums that have been paid.

Thank you.

Abbie Thornton
Enclosures

State Farm indicated that the difference in the refund amount was due to several days of coverage before cancellation. After I recalculated the number of days of coverage, State Farm still owed me money and they did not refund me the amount that was due.

V. Independent Blue Cross (IBC)

When I was working in Philadelphia, PA during 2013 and 2014, I had medical insurance with IBC. After I decided I would no longer be working in Philadelphia, I canceled my insurance.

1100 South Broad Street, #A509
Philadelphia, PA 19146
October 15, 2014

Independence Blue Cross
1901 Market Street
Philadelphia, PA 19103-1480

Subject: Cancellation of Insurance Coverage

Effective November 1, 2014, I would like to cancel my coverage due to relocating to another state.

          Member Number: 2547837600
          Group Number: 524906
          Account Number: 1754855
          Member Name: Abbie Thornton

Please send any correspondence to the following forwarding address:

          2135 Light Brigade Drive
          Matthews, NC 28105

Sincerely,

Abbie Thornton
704-622-6982

Based on my previous history in dealing with insurance companies and other organizations, I made it a habit to put all correspondences in writing. Nevertheless, IBC refunded me my premiums with no issues. See letter below:

2135 Light Brigade Drive
Matthews, NC 28105
December 1, 2014

Independence Blue Cross
Customer Service
1901 Market Street
Philadelphia, PA 19103-1480

Subject: Request for Refund – Account Number 1754855

Please submit refund in the amount of $82.58 related to the enclosed document to the following address:

        Abbie Thornton
        2135 Light Brigade Drive
        Matthews, NC 28105

Sincerely,

Abbie Thornton

Enclosure

VI. **Allstate Property and Casualty**

In 2012, after State Farm increased my homeowner's policy premiums significantly due to me having a claim in 2011 for roof damage due to hailstorm, wind, and rain, I changed to Allstate. Allstate premiums were of course much less than the increased State Farm premiums. Over the next few years, the increase in Allstate premiums were moderate and to be expected. During the 2015 premium renewal period, the increase was unreasonable. Below is a statement of my premiums for the period November 2015 to November 2016.

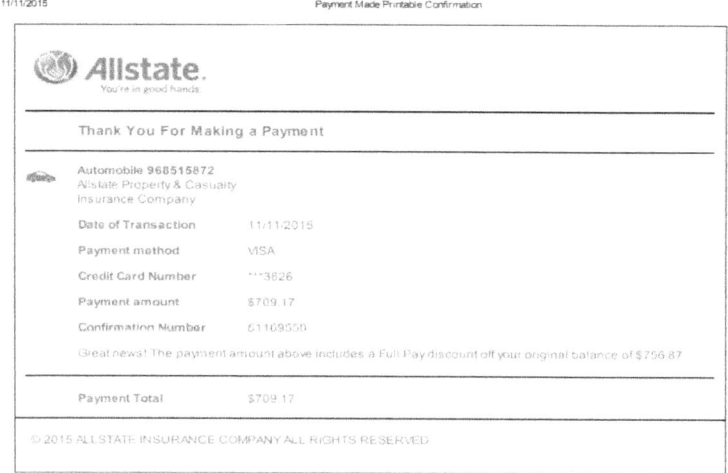

After comparing the increase in premiums from the previous years to the current year, I canceled the policy and went to Liberty Mutual for homeowners' and auto insurance coverage. See cancellation letters below:

See Letter #1:

2135 Light Brigade Drive
Matthews, North Carolina 28105
December 1, 2015

CC Parker Agency - Allstate
124 Argus Ln #C
Mooresville, NC 28117

Subject: Cancellation of Policy # 968 515 872

Please cancel policy number **968 515 872** effective December 5, 2015, and mail refund to:

Abbie Thornton
2135 Light Brigade Drive
Matthew, NC 28105

Sincerely,

[signature]

Abbie Thornton

See Letter #2:

2135 Light Brigade Drive
Matthews, NC 28105
January 10, 2016

Allstate Insurance Company
P. O. Box 660598
Dallas, TX 75266-0598

Subject: Cancellation of Policy # 968 515 872

On December 1, 2015, I requested cancellation of the above policy number through the CC Parker Agency in Mooresville, North Carolina. A second request was made on December 28, 2015.

As of today, I have not received my refund, which should effective as of December 5, 2015. Would you please ensure that my refund is mailed to the following address?

        Abbie Thornton
        2135 Light Brigade Drive
        Matthews, NC 28105

Sincerely,

Abbie Thornton

Attachment

A refund check was subsequently received from the corporate office.

VII. Liberty Mutual

During September 2018, I experienced hurricane damage at my home and was denied any coverage by Liberty Mutual. The details of this can be found in Letter 20.

As a result of the denial of my claim, I commenced to cancel all insurance with Liberty Mutual. On November 11, 2018, I canceled my auto insurance with Liberty Mutual and went with GEICO for coverage. The amount of savings with GEICO was over $400 a year.

I contacted Assurance Bankers Insurance Company on November 10, 2018 to provide me rental insurance starting 11/16/2018.

On November 11, 2018, approximately 11:15am, I called Liberty Mutual and spoke with "Alex" to cancel my renter's insurance effective 11/17/2018. My checking account was being drafted in the amount of $19.42 monthly. I checked my November 2018 bank statement to verify that the drafts had stopped, and there was no draft on the November 2018 bank statement. Based on this, I assumed that everything was processed correctly. Nevertheless, I continued to receive invoice notices indicating I had not paid my premiums of $35.74. I ignored these notices assuming their accounting system was not in sync with their customer service system. See document below:

Invoice Billing

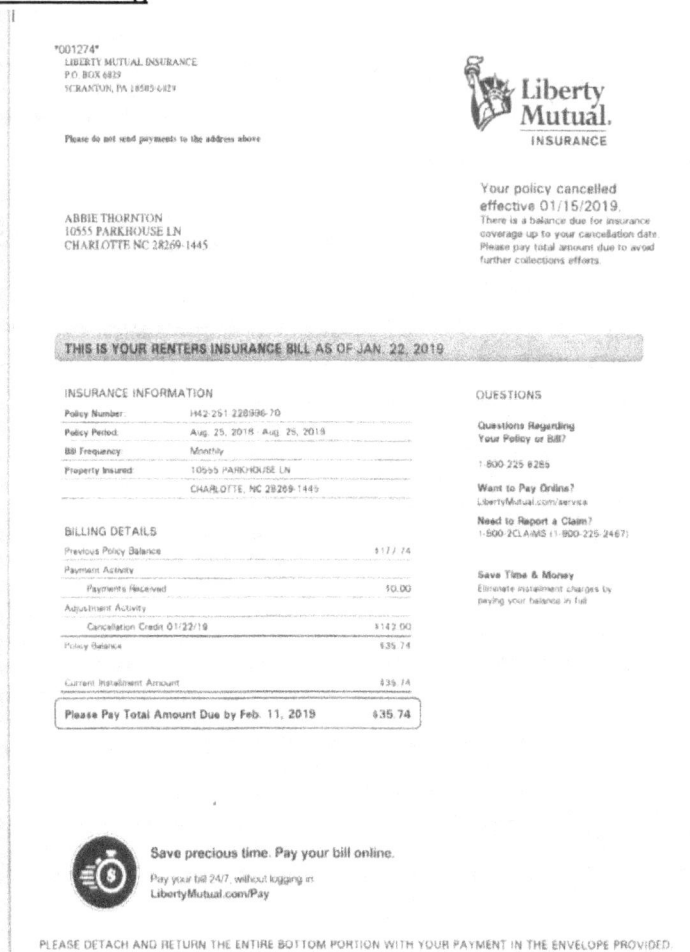

Then I received a notice from a "Credit Collection Services" dated 03/07/2019. It appears that after the drafts on my checking account was stopped, Liberty Mutual started sending me paper invoices to make premium payments. In the meantime, Liberty Mutual sent my account to a credit collection service. See document below:

Credit Collection Service

At this point I contacted Liberty Mutual by phone on 03/13/2019 regarding the policy cancellation. According to their records, I had canceled the policy 01/15/2019 instead of 11/11/2018. It appears the representative I spoke with had not followed through in completing the request for cancellation on 11/11/2018, and someone subsequently made the completion 01/15/2019. I had not communicated with Liberty Mutual after I requested that my overage be canceled on 11/11/2018.

Liberty Mutual's failure to complete my request for cancellation on a timely basis was subsequently corrected, and it resulted in me receiving a refund check in the amount of $4.26. My annual premiums went from $233 with Liberty Mutual to $169 with Assurant, savings of $64 annually. See document below:

Refund Check

I received a check dated 3/22/2021 from Liberty Mutual in the amount of $27.66. There was no explanation given for the refund.

A lot of these insurance companies have great advertising and marketing campaigns. However, their back-office practices and policies are lacking.

LETTER 20: Hurricane Florence
(Liberty Mutual Insurance Company) - September 2018

Hurricane Florence came through Charlotte North Carolina during September 14 - 18, 2018 bringing lots of rain and wind. Hurricane Michael occurred approximately three weekss later, October 10, 2018, bringing additional rain and wind to the area.

As I am standing in my garage on September 15, 2018, I see the water building up on the floor from the Sump Pump drainage overflowing. I then saw water coming in from the side of the house around the electrical panel that was on the wall in the basement garage. I went into the basement level of the house, and I smelled something burning. It was later determined that a fuse had been blown and one of the outlets had "burned out". This also caused the battery to my sump pump to explode. I noticed there was water standing in my exercise room. I immediately contacted Liberty Mutual to report a claim as the hurricane is still happening.

The next day, September 16, 2018, I was in my pool house and I notice water dripping into the pool from at least in 3-4 different areas of the roof. I then submitted another claim related to the Pool House roof damage.

I then commenced to contact contractors to provide me estimates to complete the work.

Due Diligence

On September 24, 2018, I sent an email responding to Liberty Mutual denial of my claim indicating I would be performing my own due diligence.

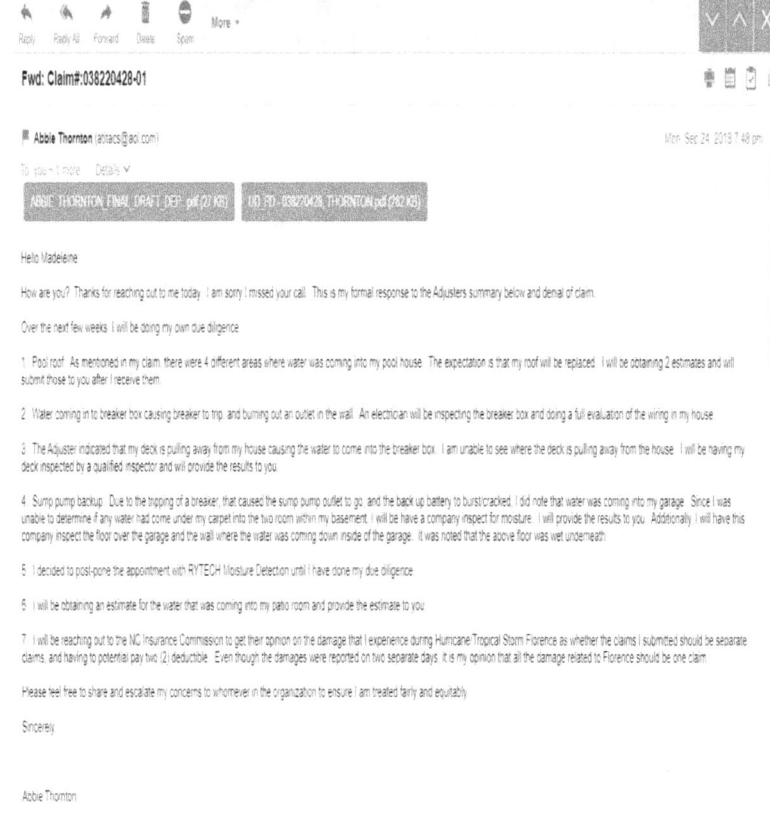

Claim Denied – 9/25/2018

On September 22, 2018, Liberty Mutual sent a Claims Representative to inspect my property and the representative subsequently denied my claims indicating that all the damages were due to normal wear and tear. See denial letter below:

September 25, 2018

Abbie Thornton
2135 Light Brigade Dr
Matthews, NC 28105-6413

Claim Number: 038220428-01
Date of Loss: 9/15/2018
Policy Number: H3225813243870
Deductible: $2,500.00

CONTACT US

By phone
Tel: (224) 806-3337
Fax: (866) 791-7490

By E-mail
ashley.glowa@libertymutual.com

Liberty Mutual Fire Insurance Company
Mailing Address:
P.O. Box 515097
Los Angeles, CA 90051-5097
Office: (866) 542-2287
Fax: (866) 791-7490

Visit us online
LibertyMutual.com

About Claims Process
Libertymutual.com/claims-center/home-insurance-claims

Dear Abbie Thorton,

At Liberty Mutual our goal is to make your claims experience as easy and worry-free as possible. I'm writing you now to share the latest information about your homeowners claim.

As we recently discussed, I have reviewed your claim for wind driven rain from roof and wind driven rain from back porch pulling away from back elevation wall to the garage drywall and braker causing shortout to the family room circuit, wind driven rain to the sunroom window trim and seeping onto the ceramic tile. Then wind driven rain through the ridge cap on pool house roof dripping into the pool then water going under the pool house causing creases in pool liner. I've also shared with you an estimate for the damage that is covered by your policy.

Results of the Review
After reviewing all the current facts and the terms of your policy, I have determined we are unable to issue you a payment for the damage(s). There are two reasons for this:

1. Your deductible is more than the damage covered by your policy.
2. Your policy does not cover wear and tear and/or deterioration to the roof, settling to the back deck, and surface/ground water to the pool liner.

Your Policy
I know this can be disappointing news, so I want to make sure you fully understand the reason for this outcome. With that in mind, here's the section of your policy that pertains to wear and tear and/or deterioration, settling, and surface/ground water.

SECTION I – PERILS INSURED AGAINST

COVERAGE A – DWELLING and COVERAGE B – OTHER STRUCTURES
We insure against risk of direct loss to property described in Coverages A and B only if that loss is a physical loss to property. We do not insure, however, for loss:
2. Caused by:
 e Any of the following:
  (3) Any cracking, bulging, sagging, bending, leaning, settling, shrinkage or expansion as such condition relates to (1) or (2) above; except as provided in E.8. Collapse under Section I – Property Coverages; or
  (6) Any of the following:
   (a) Wear and tear, marring, deterioration.

UD_PD

Page 1 of 3

(b) Mechanical breakdown, latent defect, inherent vice or any quality in property that causes it to damage or destroy itself

If any of these cause water damage not otherwise excluded, from a plumbing, heating, air conditioning or automatic fire protective sprinkler system or household appliance, we cover loss caused by the water including the cost of tearing out and replacing any part of a building necessary to repair the system or appliance. We do not cover loss to the system or appliance from which this water escaped.

SECTION I – EXCLUSIONS

A. We do not insure for loss caused directly or indirectly by any of the following. Such loss is excluded regardless of any other cause or event contributing concurrently or in any sequence to the loss. These exclusions apply whether or not the loss event results in widespread damage or affects a substantial area.

3. Water
This means:
a) Flood, surface water, waves, including tidal wave and tsunami, tides, tidal water, overflow of any body of water, or spray from any of these, all whether or not driven by wind, including storm surge;
c) Water below the surface of the ground, including water which exerts pressure on, or seeps, leaks or flows through a building, sidewalk, patio, foundation, swimming pool or other structure; or

Your Next Steps

- To protect your property, please begin the repair process as soon as possible. If you don't have a preferred contractor, I can recommend one in your area.

- If you do have a preferred contractor, please make sure they email me their estimate (if different from the Liberty Mutual estimate), along with any photos, prior to starting any repairs.

- During repairs, the contractor may find additional damage that wasn't included in the initial estimate. If this happens, please call me before the work begins, as all additional work must be pre-approved by Liberty Mutual.

Here to Help

If you have any questions, or any new information to share, please email or call me. I can assist you more quickly if you reference your claim number in all communications.

Thank you for trusting Liberty Mutual with all your Insurance needs.

UD_PD

Sincerely,

Ashley Gliwa
Your Liberty Mutual Claims Team

Update on Due Diligence
On October 8, 2018, I wrote the following letter to give Liberty Mutual representatives an update of my due diligence.

2135 Light Brigade Drive
Matthews, NC 28105
October 8, 2018

Subject: Claim 038220428-01

As I mentioned in the email I sent on 09/23/18 that over the next few weeks, I will be doing my own due diligence. Below is the status of the follow-up to the email.

1. Pool roof. As mentioned in my claim, there were 4 different areas where water was coming into my pool house. The expectation is that my roof will be replaced. I will be obtaining 2 estimates and will submit those to you after I receive them.

    I have attached two (2) separate quotes/proposals for the replacement of the roof. See files referenced below:

    a) Abbie Thornton Roof Job - McCray Builders.doc
    b) Rob_Proposal – SHS Pros Roofing.pdf

2. Water coming in to breaker box causing breaker to trip and burning out an outlet in the wall. An electrician will be inspecting the breaker box and doing a full evaluation of the wiring in my house.

    Mister Sparky Electrician performed a safety inspection on 9/28/18. They have presented 3 options. Option #3 is the safety minimum. See files referenced below:

    a) Mr Sparky Wise Electric – Options
    b) Mr. Sparky Wise Electric - Receipt

3. The Adjuster indicated that my deck is pulling away from my house causing the water to come into the breaker box. I am unable to see where the deck is pulling away from the house. I will be having my deck inspected by a qualified inspector and will provide the results to you.

    On 10/5/18, your structural engineer did an inspection and he should be giving you his report from his inspection regarding the deck pulling away from my house. He mentioned briefly that it may be a flashing problem.

4. Sump pump backup: Due to the tripping of a breaker, that caused the sump pump outlet to go out that was on the same breaker as the outlet that burned-out, and the back-up battery to burst/cracked, I did note that water was coming into my garage. Since I was unable to determine if any water had come under my carpet into the two room within my basement, I will be having a company inspect for moisture. I will provide the results to you.

    On 10/4/18 Moisture Loc visited my home and did not find any moisture in the basement. See document reference below for back-up battery replacement for sump pump.

    a) Invoice for battery installation
    b) Battery Receipt - Sump Pump

Additionally, I will have this company inspect the floor over the garage and the wall where the water was coming down inside of the garage. It was noted that the above floor was wet underneath.

a) I will wait to hear the results from your structural engineer/inspector that visited my home on 10/5/18.

5. I decided to post-pone the appointment with RYTECH Moisture Detection until I have done my due diligence.
NA

6. I will be obtaining an estimate for the water that was coming into my patio room and provide the estimate to you.

Attached is the estimate for repair work in the patio room. See file referenced below:

a) AbbieThornton_92718-Ask Hand Inc. (work is currently in progress)

7. I will be reaching out to the NC Insurance Commission to get their opinion on the damage that I experience during Hurricane/Tropical Storm Florence as to whether the claims I submitted should be separate claims and having to potential pay two (2) deductible. Even though the damages were reported on two separate days, it is my opinion that all the damage related to Florence should be one claim.

Thanks for your clarification on the claims being consolidated into one claim.

Sincerely,

Abbie Thornton

If Liberty Mutual will not honor their policy, I am requesting a refund of all premiums I have paid over the last 3 years, which totals $4,874.00.

November 9, 2018 Correspondences

After indicating that I did not agree with the Claim Representative's assessment and denial of claim, and deciding to get my own assessment, Liberty Mutual contracted with Rimkus Engineering. I am aware that he was hired to come up with the same conclusions the Liberty Mutual Claims Representative came up with. I know how this process works, Liberty Mutual is paying him. After receiving the report from Rimkus Engineer, I responded with the following email.

Re: Rimkus Report of Findings, Insured: Abbie Thornton, Claim #: 038220428, RCG #: 00507988 Claim#:038220428-01

Abbie Thornton atntacs@aol.com Hide ∨   Fri, Nov 9, 2018 11:24 am

To: Ashley.Gilwa@LibertyMutual.com
Cc: RONALD.RICE@LibertyMutual.com, madeleine.murray@libertymutual.com, ATTTACS@aol.com, tmtoddlaw@aol.com

Hello Everyone,

After reviewing the '**Report of findings**' and the '**Denial of Claims**', I will be proceeding with the repairs of damage to my home as a result of Hurricane Florence, and will be submitting the receipts for reimbursement to the President of Liberty Mutual, as well as expressing my concerns.

If necessary, I will be formally filing a complaint against Liberty Mutual with the North Department of Insurance and the Better Business Bureau. My goal will be to have Liberty Mutual's license rescinded from doing business in the state of North Carolina. Also, I will be requesting a refund of all the premiums I have paid Liberty Mutual in the last 2-3 years for all of my policies.

When a home that is in need of some repair is totally destroyed by wind, does Liberty Mutual conclude that the home collapsed because it needed to be repaired, and the claim is denied? Does Liberty Mutual do an inspection of a home before they insures the home?

In essence, the insurance coverage I am receiving is "NOTHING"

One of the reasons I selected Liberty Mutual for all of my insurance needs, was because your brand was very positive and appeared to be fair. Let's not change that image. Thanks for your attention.

Abbie Thornton

Letter to Liberty President and NC Insurance Commissioner

After several months had passed and on March 5, 2019, I decided to write a letter to the President of Liberty Mutual requesting that I be reimbursed for the expenses I had incurred to repair the damages that resulted from Hurricanes Florence and Michael. See letter below:

2135 Light Brigade Drive
Matthews, NC 28105
March 5, 2019

Mr. David H. Long, Chairman /CEO
Liberty Mutual Insurance
175 Berkeley Street
Boston, Massachusetts 02116

Subject: Claim 038220428-01 Request for Reimbursement

The purpose of this letter is to request that I be reimbursed for expenses incurred ($9,767.44) as a result of repair damages that were made from the Florence Hurricane that occurred September 14- 18, 2018 and Hurricane Michael that occurred October 10, 2018. My claim was denied by your Claims Department indicating damages were due to normal wear and tear.

Below is a summary for your information:

September 15, 2018: I submitted a claim (0382204428) to Liberty Mutual regarding damages that I notice within my house as the storm was occurring.

September 16, 2018: I submitted a second claim (038222944) of damages that I noticed while vacuuming my enclosed pool. The pool was leaking in four (4) different areas.

September 17, 2018: I was contacted by Madeleine Murray, Claims Representative to obtain more detail regarding the claims. I send Madeleine various picture regarding the damages. Below are some of the pictures submitted:

- Attachment 1 – Pictures of water in Patio Room
- Attachment 2 – Pictures of water in Garage from Sump Pump backup
- Attachment 3 – Pictures of Pool House Roof

September 18, 2018: I was contacted by Ashley Gliwa, Claims Resolution Specialist II to discuss my claims and to schedule a visit to the property. Ashley indicated that the claims would be treated separately and that two (2) separate deductibles would have to be applied. Claim 038222944 was subsequently withdrawn and merged with claim 0382204428, but it was still indicated that I would have to pay two (2) deductibles. (Attachment 4)

I disagreed with Ashley indicating that even though the two claims were filed on different days, they are the result of Hurricane Florence damages. After further discussion and differing of opinions, I indicated that I would contact the NC Department of Insurance to get their opinion regarding the two claims.

September 22, 2018: Ashley Gliwa inspected my property on 9/22/18 and subsequently submitted a denial of claim indicating that the damages were due to "wear and tear". I contacted Madeleine Murray, Claims Representative to let her know that the findings from Ashley Gliwa, Claims Resolution Specialist II were unacceptable and that I will be doing my own due diligence.

September 24,2018: I responded to the Claims Adjuster (Ashley Gliwa, Claims Resolution Specialist II) denial of my claim. (Attachment 5)

September 26, 2018: Liberty Mutual sent me a "Reservation of Rights" because I did not agree with the assessment made by the Claims Agent. (Attachment 6)

September 27, 2018: The leak in the Sunroom was repaired by ASK HAND Handyman, $852.64, to prevent additional damages. As you are aware, a second hurricane (Michael) hit North Carolina a few weeks later, October 10, 2018. (Attachment G)

October 5, 2018: After I indicated I would be doing my own due diligence, Liberty Mutual sent their representative (Rimkus Engineering Company) to my home to perform additional inspections.

October 8, 2018: The following is the status update to the email that I sent to Liberty Mutual (Madeline Murray), on 9/24/18 responding to their claim denial.

> As I mentioned in the e-mail, I sent on 9/24/18 that over the next few weeks, I will be doing my own due diligence. Below is the status of the follow-up to the email.
>
> 1. Pool roof: As mentioned in my claim, there were 4 different areas where water was coming into my pool house. The expectation is that my roof will be replaced. I will be obtaining 2 estimates and will submit those to you after I receive them.
>
>   *I have attached two (2) separate quotes/proposals for the replacement of the roof. See files referenced below:*
>
>   a) *Abbie Thornton Roof Job - McCray Builders.doc* (Attachment A)
>   b) *Rob_Proposal – SHS Pros Roofing.pdf* (Attachment B)
>
> 2. Water coming in to breaker box causing breaker to trip and burning out an outlet in the wall. An electrician will be inspecting the breaker box and doing a full evaluation of the wiring in my house.
>
>   *Mister Sparky Electrician performed a safety inspection on 9/28/18. They have presented 3 options. Option #3 is the safety minimum. See files referenced below:*
>
>   a) *Mr Sparky Wise Electric – Options* (Attachment C)
>   b) *Mr. Sparky Wise Electric – Receipt, 9/28/18 $79.00* (Attachment D)
>
> 3. The Adjuster indicated that my deck is pulling away from my house causing the water to come into the breaker box. I am unable to see where the deck is pulling away from the house. I will be having my deck inspected by a qualified inspector and will provide the results to you.
>
>   *On 10/5/18, your structural engineer did an inspection and he should be giving you his report from his inspection regarding the deck pulling away from my house. He mentioned briefly that it may be a flashing problem.*
>
> 4. Sump pump backup: Due to the tripping of a breaker, that caused the sump pump outlet to go out that was on the same breaker as the outlet that burned-out, and caused the back-up battery to burst/cracked, I did note that water was coming into my garage. Since I was unable to determine if any water had come under my carpet into the two room within my basement, I will be having a company inspect for moisture. I will provide the results to you.
>
>   *On 10/4/18 Moisture Loc visited my home and did not find any moisture in the basement. See document reference below for back-up battery replacement for sump pump.*
>
>   a) *Invoice for battery installation, 9/19/18 $50.00*   (Attachment E)
>   b) *Battery Receipt - Sump Pump, 9/19/18 $85.80*   (Attachment F)
>
>   *Additionally, I will have this company inspect the floor over the garage and the wall where the water was coming down inside of the garage. It was noted that the above floor was wet underneath.*

a) I will wait to hear the results from your structural engineer/inspector that visited my home on 10/5/18.

5. I decided to post-pone the appointment with RYTECH Moisture Detection until I have done my due diligence.

    NA

6. I will be obtaining an estimate for the water that was coming into my patio room and provide the estimate to you.

    Attached is the estimate for repair work in the patio room. See file referenced below:

    a) AbbieThornton_92718-Ask Hand Inc. (work is currently in progress)   (Attachment G)

7. I will be reaching out to the NC Insurance Commission to get their opinion on the damage that I experience during Hurricane/Tropical Storm Florence as to whether the claims I submitted should be separate claims and having to potential pay two (2) deductible. Even though the damages were reported on two separate days, it is my opinion that all the damage related to Florence should be one claim.

    Thanks for your decision on the claims being consolidated into one claim, and one deductible.

October 10, 2018: Hurricane Michael hit North Carolina and Charlotte experienced substantial rainfall.

November 11, 2018: Approximately 5 weeks later, Rimkus Engineering submitted their assessment to Liberty Mutual agreeing with the initial assessment of Ashley Gliwa, Claims Resolution Specialist II indicating damages were due to "wear and tear". I am convinced that Rimkus Engineering is not independent of Liberty Mutual. I am also aware that insurance companies incent their claims agents to find ways to deny claims.

November 19, 2018: I send an email to Ronald Rice, Ashley Gliwa, Madeleine Murray indicating that I would be proceeding with the repair of damages to my home and that I would be submitting receipt for reimbursement to the President of Liberty Mutual.

November 26, 2018: The roof on the pool house was replaced by McCray Builders, $8,700.00. Several pieces of plywood had to be replaced. The original roof was installed in 2007 and the average life of a room is from 20 to 30 years.   (Attachment H)

CONCLUSION: The facts are that as a result of Hurricane Florence, I experienced the damages that are highlighted in this letter, and I incurred the costs highlighted in "blue". It is disturbing to be told that in the midst of a major storm, and seeing water coming into my home that this is due to "**normal wear and tear**". If this is Liberty Mutual philosophy, then it should only ensure new homes (one year old or less).

I have been insured with Liberty Mutual since 2016, policy number H32-258-132438-70. Based on your advertisement, it appeared that Liberty Mutual's brand was an honesty, morality and care; and that their ensured best interest was number one.

I appreciate Liberty Mutual upholding their end of the contract to provide coverage for my home in the event of damages/disaster; and reimburse me for the $9,767.44 of damages incurred and paid by me as a result of Hurricane Florence.

Sincerely,

Abbie Thornton
License# 5799673

CC: James F. Kelleher, Executive VP and Chief Legal Officer – Liberty Mutual
      Mike Causey, North Carolina Department of Insurance Commissioner
      The Law Offices of T. Michael Todd

Attachments

Below are the attachments that were included with the above letter.

Attachment 1: Water in basement

Attachment 2: Water in garage

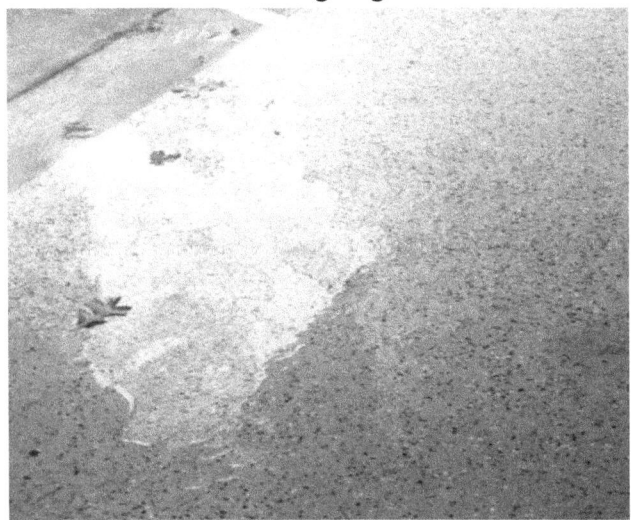

Attachment 3: Pool house

Attachment 4: Two Deductibles

Hi Ms. Tharton,

I have withdrawn this claim for claim# 038222944 since we discussed about the other claim# 038220428 having been made that included all of the losses to your home. I have discussed the 2 separate losses to your home such as the sump pump failure from the water leaking on the breakers causing a power failure plus the water damages to your sun room. Then the roof damage to your pool roof. Based on our discussion, this will to under one claim with 2 separate deductibles - 1 for the sump pump back up environment and the other under your dwelling coverage.

Please let me know if you have any further questions. I look forward to meeting with you on Saturday, 9/22 at 8am.

Thank you

Attachment 5: Due Diligence

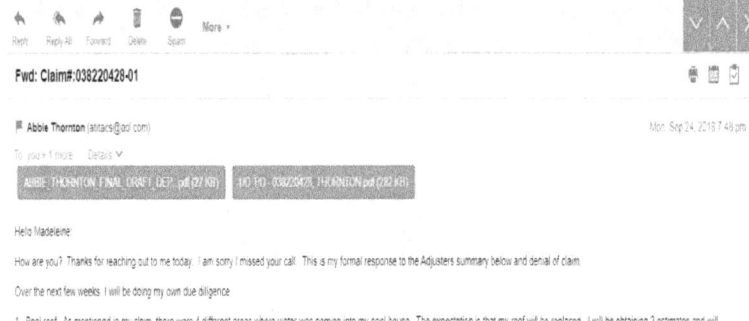

Fwd: Claim#:038220428-01

Abbie Thornton (ahtars@aol.com)   Mon, Sep 24, 2018 7:48 pm

To you + 1 more   Details ∨

[ABBIE THORNTON FINAL DRAFT GEJI..pdf (92 KB)] [WO TO - 038220828_THORNSON.pdf (282 KB)]

Hello Madeleine:

How are you? Thanks for reaching out to me today. I am sorry I missed your call. This is my formal response to the Adjusters summary below and denial of claim.

Over the next few weeks I will be doing my own due diligence.

1. Pool roof: As mentioned in my claim, there were 4 different areas where water was coming into my pool house. The expectation is that my roof will be replaced. I will be obtaining 2 estimates and will submit those to you after I receive them.

2. Water coming in to breaker box causing breaker to trip, and burning out an outlet in the wall. An electrician will be inspecting the breaker box and doing a full evaluation of the wiring in my house.

3. The Adjuster indicated that my deck is pulling away from my house causing the water to come into the breaker box. I am unable to see where the deck is pulling away from the house. I will be having my deck inspected by a qualified inspector and will provide the results to you.

4. Sump pump backup: Due to the tripping of a breaker that caused the sump pump outlet to go, and the back up battery to burst/cracked. I did note that water was coming into my garage. Since I was unable to determine if any water had come under my carpet into the two room within my basement, I will be have a company inspect for moisture. I will provide the results to you. Additionally, I will have this company inspect the floor over the garage and the wall where the water was coming down inside of the garage. It was noted that the above floor was wet underneath.

5. I decided to post-pone the appointment with RYTECH Moisture Detection until I have done my due diligence.

6. I will be obtaining an estimate for the water that was coming into my patio room and provide the estimate to you.

7. I will be reaching out to the NC Insurance Commission to get their opinion on the damage that I experience during Hurricane/Tropical Storm Florence as whether the claims I submitted should be separate claims, and having to potential pay two (2) deductible. Even though the damages were reported on two separate days, it is my opinion that all the damage related to Florence should be one claim.

Please feel free to share and escalate my concerns to whomever in the organization to ensure I am treated fairly and equitably.

Sincerely,

Abbie Thornton

Attachment 6: Reservation of Rights

September 26, 2018

Abbie Thornton
2135 Light Brigade Dr
Matthews NC 28105-6413

Claim Number: HD000-038220428-01
Date of Loss: 09/15/2018

Dear Abbie Thornton,

Please be advised this letter is in regard to the investigation of the above captioned claim for damage due to Hurricane/Tropical Storm.

We are investigating this loss under a reservation of all rights under the policy and applicable law. This letter should not be construed as a waiver or estoppel of any of the terms, conditions, or defenses afforded by the policy or applicable law, and nothing herein shall be deemed to be either an admission or denial of liability. While we are not waiving any of our rights, we also understand that you are retaining and reserving your rights as well.

No decision on your claim has been made, and a "reservation of rights" is not a claims decision or denial. We are in the fact-gathering stage, and when a decision has been made we will contact you to discuss your claim.

Thank you again for choosing to insure with Liberty Mutual. While the investigation of your claim continues, please do not hesitate to contact me if you have any questions or concerns, either by phone or by email, at your convenience. When contacting me by email, please include your claim number in the subject line.

Sincerely,
Madeleine Murray
Homeowner Claims Department

CONTACT US

By Phone
Direct: (972) 808-4350
Toll Free: (800) 225-2467
Ext. 26750

By E-mail
madeleine.murray@
libertymutual.com

Liberty Mutual Fire Insurance Company
P.O. Box 515097
Los Angeles, CA 90051-5097

Visit us online
LibertyMutual.com

About Claims Process
Libertymutual.com/claims
insurance/about-claims-process

Mobile
Scan QR Code with your iPhone or Android smartphone to download the claims app or download a free reader app at www.xxxgma.mobi

Attachment A: *Proposal*

 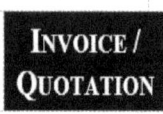

MCCRAY BUILDERS
Jim McCray
7309 Conifer Circle
Indian Trail, NC 28079
(704) 882-0908

INVOICE / QUOTATION

TO: ABBIE THORNTON
2135 LIGHT BRIGADE DRIVE
MATTHEWS, NC 28105
PH. (704) 622-6982

DATE: September 14, 2020

WE ARE PLEASED TO QUOTE YOU AS FOLLOWS: YOUR INQUIRY: $6,000.00

Terms: In Full After Completion

DESCRIPTION	AMOUNT
ESTIMATE-POOL HOUSE ONLY	
TO FURNISH LABOR AND MATERIAL TO STRIP ROOF OFF DOWN TO THE BOARDING AND THEN REPLACE WITH:	
15# FELT UNDERLAYMENT	
30YR. LAMINATED SHINGLES A.R.	
FLASH (4) SKY LITES	
CONTINUOUS RIDGE VENTILATION	
CHANGE OUT (4) SKY LITES @ $500.00 EACH	$2,000.00
TOP CHORD TRUSS REPAIR	$200.00
TO PROTECT SHRUBS, FLOWERS, AND LANDSCAPING DURING TEAR OFF. TO CLEAN UP AND HAUL AWAY ALL JOB RELATED DEBRIS.	
PAYMENT: IN FULL AFTER CLEAN UP AND JOB ARE	

ABOVE PRICES GOOD FOR ____ DAYS   SIGNATURE _____

Attachment B: Proposal

Proposal

Date: 9/27/2018

9307 Monroe Road Ste O
Charlotte, North Carolina 28270
Phone: (704) 531-2122
Website: www.shspros.com
NC General Contractor Licence #: 68186

Abbie Thornton
2135 Light Brigade Drive
Matthews, NC 28105
Ph: (704) 622-6982
atirtacs@aol.com

Product	Description	Total
Material Removal	Removal of 1 layer of existing shingles, underlayment, and all other job debris. SHS will protect landscaping with tarps and utilize a magnetic rake to remove all nails. SHS will inspect roof decking and replace 7/16" OSB decking at an additional $60 per sheet, 1/2" CDX plywood at an additional $70 per sheet, or 1"x6" decking at an additional $5.50 per foot. PLEASE NOTE: Your attic will have sawdust, debris and possibly a few roofing nails on the floor during the installation process. If your attic is accessible, you may want to cover the floor and belongings with plastic or a tarp. Also, any unsecured of valuable pictures or articles on your walls should be set down for the duration of the project.	$ 693.00
GAF Tiger Paw	Installation of GAF Tiger Paw synthetic underlayment with 1" button cap nails.	$ 330.00
Drip Edge - 1 1/2"	SHS will install 1 1/2" aluminum drip edge to all eaves.	$ 210.00
GAF WeatherWatch	Installation of GAF WeatherWatch ice and water shield to valleys and penetrations.	$ 82.50
GAF ProStart	Installation of GAF ProStart starter shingles to all eaves and rakes.	$ 121.00
GAF Timberline High Definition	Installation of GAF Timberline High Definition architectural shingles with 1 1/4" Electro-Galvanized nails. GAF Timberline High Definition shingles take 3 bundles to cover 100 square feet (1 Square).	$ 3,970.00
GAF Cobra III	Installation of GAF Cobra III ridge vent to all ridges.	$ 385.00
GAF Seal-A-Ridge	Installation of GAF Seal-A-Ridge hip and ridge shingles.	$ 181.50
1 1/4" EG Nails	Shingles will be installed with 1 1/4" Electro-galvanized nails.	$ 38.50
1" Button Cap Nails	Underlayment will be installed with 1" button cap nails.	$ 33.00
NP-1 Roof Sealant	Installation of NP-1 roof sealant to all aluminum flashing, exposed fasteners, and all other necessary areas to ensure a waterproof job.	$ 8.25
Velux	Installation of 6 Velux Skylights and flashing kits	$ 5,700.00
Osb	Installation of one sheet of OSB plywood to rotted piece on Roof. Painting underside white before installation	$ 22.00
2"x4"	Scab on 2"x4" to rotted rafter. Painting 2"x4" white prior to installation. Homeowner to supply paint	$ 12.00
Discount	Discount	$ -700.00
GAF Silver Pledge Warranty	AS A GAF CERTIFIED MASTER ELITE CONTRACTOR, SHS WILL REGISTER YOUR WARRANTY FOR GAF'S SILVER PLEDGE WARRANTY. THIS EXTENDS THE WARRANTY FROM 10 YEARS OF NON-PRORATED COVERAGE TO 50 YEARS OF NON-PRORATED COVERAGE. IT COVERS ALL MATERIALS, LABOR, TEAR-OFF, AND DISPOSAL. IT ALSO COVERS WORKMANSHIP FOR A PERIOD OF 10 YEARS. ADD $10 PER SQUARE TO UPGRADE TO GAF'S GOLDEN PLEDGE WARRANTY WHICH COVERS WORKMANSHIP FOR 25 YEARS.	$ 0.00
Workmanship Warranty	WORKMANSHIP WARRANTY. SOUTHERN HOME SERVICES, LLC WILL WARRANTY ALL INSTALLED MATERIALS FROM INSTALLATION DEFECTS FOR THE PERIOD OF 5 YEARS. NOTE: ANY ALTERATIONS MADE BY OTHERS WILL VOID THIS WARRANTY.	$ 0.00
Financing	FINANCING AVAILABLE THROUGH ENERBANK AND SYNCHRONY.	$ 0.00
Payment Terms	A 25% DOWN PAYMENT IS REQUIRED AT THE TIME OF QUOTE ACCEPTANCE. THE BALANCE WILL BE DUE UPON COMPLETION OF THE PROJECT.	$ 0.00

Roof color: _____

We at Southern Home Services, LLC ("SHS") want this to by a seamless experience for all involved parties. This list has been prepared for that exact reason. If you have any questions or concerns, please contact us at 704-531-2122.

• Dates you request that work NOT be done.

_____

• Do you have Outside electrical outlets?

_____

Scheduling of the jobs may vary due to weather. Please be aware that 2 days of unsatisfactory weather could push back your job up to 1 days.
• Do you have any delicate plants or other property of concern that are near the home?

Project Details		$ 0.00
	If yes where?	

- Make sure all animals are safe in the house while we are working on your home.
- Your satellite dish may need to be removed and reset unless told otherwise. Your cable company or satellite provider may need to fix your signal when the job is complete.

- SHS will remove all patio furniture from the patio deck area. Are there any special instructions? _____

- Make sure anything hanging on the walls are secured or removed before we start your project.
- Your attic may accumulate sawdust or nails on the floor during normal construction activities. If your attic is accessible, you may want to cover the floor or belongings with plastic or a tarp.

- Please park vehicles on the street until the end of day clean up

- Material drop location: _____

Subtotal	$ 10,986.75
Sales Tax	$ 0.00
Total	$ 10,986.75

Thank you for the opportunity to earn your business. Please contact me directly with questions or to accept this proposal.

Rob Drumm
Project Consultant
Rob@shspros.com
Office: 704-531-2122
Mobile: 704-622-5335

Attachment C: Electrical Inspection

704-297-0846

Mister Sparky

525 North Tryon St.
Suite 1600
Charlotte, NC 28202
www.mistersparkycharlotte.com

A Division Of WISE

1242 Shelby Hwy
P.O. Box 1122
Cherryville, NC 28021
fax (704) 435-1957
www.cherryville.mistersparky.com

1-888-823-3060

No More Malarky, Call Mister Sparky!

Job Number: 35076 Tech Name: Jordan [illegible]

Customer Name: Abbie Thornton

Phone: [illegible] Date: 9-28-18

Additional Job Notes/Instructions:

Option 1) Premier Volt Vault
[illegible]
all [illegible]
Arc fault protection

$14,077

Option 2) Basic Volt Vault
[illegible] arc fault

- New Panel
- New Breakers $[illegible] (recommended)
- Surge protection
- Update grounding system
- [illegible]
- Panel torque • [illegible]

Option 3) Panel [illegible] and [illegible]
(Safety [illegible])

- Replace all breakers
- [illegible] $1908
- [illegible]
- [illegible]
- Panel torque
- Label

Thank you very much for your business!

Please call if you have any questions about the work we have completed or estimated for you. Estimates are only valid for a limited time.

Attachment D: Electrical Invoice

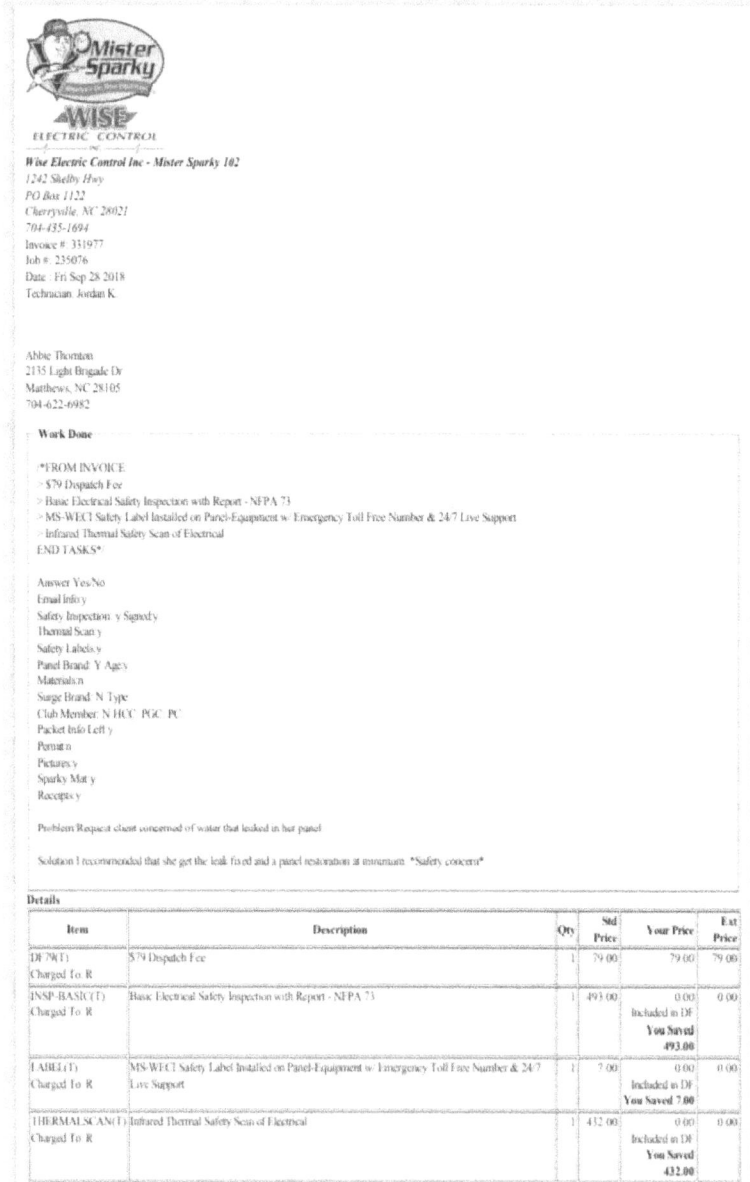

	Total	79.00
	Payment Amount	79.00

Payment Details

Payment Method:	Visa
Name on Card	Abbie thornton
Authorization Number	AY0A0EF9E38E

Thank You and No More Malarky!
Thank you for choosing Mister Sparky by Wise Electric Control Inc.! It's our pleasure to serve you! "No More Malarky, You Called Mister Sparky!"

How did we do today?
Give us a review and a chance to win $100! Answer 3 quick questions here: https://client-voice.com/mistersparky

Children's Miracle Network Partner
We are a proud partner with the Levine Children's Hospital of Charlotte NC - your contribution is greatly appreciated - please retain this receipt for your records.

Find us on FACEBOOK & TWITTER!!
FACEBOOK is "Mister Sparky by Wise Electric Control Inc." and TWITTER is @MisterSparkyNC

Cancellation Policy
Cancellation, Return & Refund Policy: All priority and prepaid dispatch fees are non-refundable once booked. All authorized work or product is subject to a 25% service fee if cancelled or returned. Cancellations must be in writing and acknowledged to be valid. Refunds are given on a 30 day period via check.

Customer Supplied Equipment
All Customer Supplied Equipment is the responsibility of the customer including equipment warranty, labor, diagnostic and travel costs incurred by improper, damaged, or failed equipment.

Payment Policy
All work requires immediate COD payment upon completion. Any unpaid balance after completion of work is subject to an additional 25% admin fee at completion date and at every 30 days past due

Warranty
Unless otherwise specified by manufacturer, all repairs have a FULL 3 year parts and labor warranty.

NC Gen. Stat.
As per NC Gen. Stat. 105-164.4(a)(16) & 105-164.3(33g) some items including labor may be taxed at State and County tax rates.

Office Locations:
CHARLOTTE: 525 North Tryon St, Suite 1600, Charlotte NC 28202 | CHERRYVILLE: 1242 Shelby Hwy, PO Box 1122, Cherryville NC 28021

I authorize the above work to be completed and I agree to pay the above total.

I agree that the above work was completed to my satisfaction and I agree to pay the above total.

Attachment E: Battery Replacement and Installation

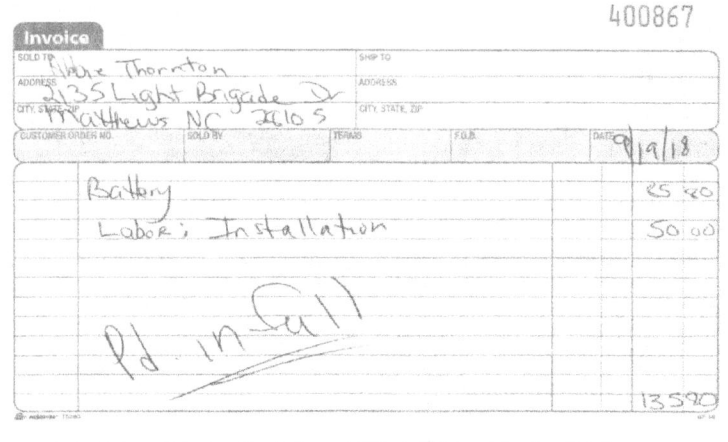

Attachment F: Battery Receipt

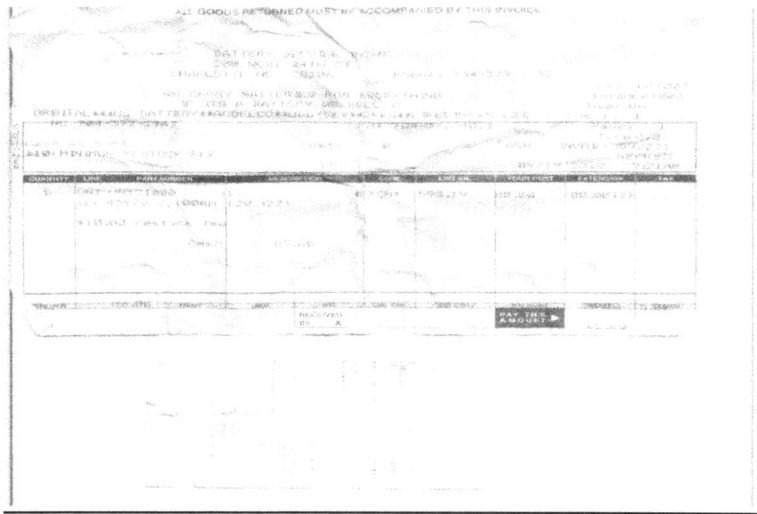

Attachment G: Basement repairs

ASK HAND HANDYMAN

3495 Monarch Court SW
Concord, NC 28027
704-561-1652

QUOTE

QUOTE #	DATE
92701	9/27/18

FOR
Abbie Thornton
2135 Light Brigade Drive
Matthews, NC 28105

REF	TERMS
	Good for 30 Days

DESCRIPTION	QTY	UNIT PRICE	AMOUNT
Repair Wood - bottom-right of porch window	1	175	
Repair Wood - soffit and side board, upper level	1	$170.00	
Check, Realign, and Secure Suspected Problem Gutters	1	150	
Repair Wood - trim inside porch	1	60	
Inspect and Recaulk along outside	1	120	
Paint All Repaired Wood - Gloss White Paint	1	$120.00	

Make all checks payable to Ask Hand, Inc.

SUBTOTAL	$795.00
TAX RATE	0725
TAX	$57.64
TOTAL	$852.64

If you have any questions concerning this quote, please contact us at:
704-561-1652 • ibd@askhand.com
Thank you for your consideration!

Attachment H: Invoice on Roof Replacement

MCCRAY BUILDERS
Jim McCray
7309 Conifer Circle
Indian Trail, NC 28079
(704) 882-0908

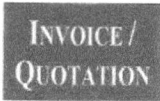

TO: ABBIE THORNTON
2135 LIGHT BRIGADE DRIVE
MATTHEWS, NC 28105
PH: (704) 822-6982

DATE: November 27, 2018

WE ARE PLEASED TO QUOTE YOU AS FOLLOWS: YOUR INQUIRY **$8,700.00**

Terms: In Full After Completion

DESCRIPTION	AMOUNT
ESTIMATE-POOL HOUSE ONLY	
TO FURNISH LABOR AND MATERIAL TO STRIP ROOF OFF DOWN TO THE BOARDING AND THEN REPLACE WITH:	
15# FELT UNDERLAYMENT	
30YR LAMINATED SHINGLES A.R.	
FLASH AND CHANGE OUT (4) SKY LITES	
CONTINUOUS RIDGE VENTILATION	
ALUMINUM DRIP EDGE AROUND PERIMETER	
VINYL GUTTER GUARD ALONG BOTH EAVES	
TOP CHORD TRUSS REPAIR	
TO PROTECT SHRUBS, FLOWERS, AND LANDSCAPING DURING TEAR OFF. TO CLEAN UP AND HAUL AWAY ALL JOB RELATED DEBRIS.	
MCCRAY BUILDERS TO WARRANT ROOF FOR 1 YEAR LABOR AND MATERIAL AND OWENS CORNING TO WARRANT SHINGLES FOR 30 YEAR PRO-RATED	
PAID IN FULL CHECK # 9914 11/26/18 THANK YOU!	

ABOVE PRICES GOOD FOR _____ DAYS   SIGNATURE _____

A copy of the above letter was sent by certified mail to NC Insurance Commissioner, Mike Causey and the President of Liberty Mutual David H. Long. See documents below:

September 18, 2018

Abbie Thornton
2135 Light Brigade Dr
Matthews, NC 28105-6413

Claim Number: 038222944-01
Date of Loss: 9/16/2018

Dear Abbie Thornton,

CONTACT US

By phone
Tel: (224) 806-3337

Fax: (866) 791-7490

By E-mail
ashley.gliwa@libertymutual.com

Liberty Mutual Fire Insurance Company

Mailing Address:
P.O. Box 515097
Los Angeles, CA 90051-5097
Office: (866) 542-2287
Fax: (866) 791-7490

Visit us online
LibertyMutual.com

About Claims Process
Libertymutual.com/claims-center/home-insurance-claims

Liberty Mutual Insurance appreciates the opportunity to be of service to you, especially during this time. Our goal is to provide you with exceptional customer service to ensure we are meeting your specific needs.

Per your request, your claim has been closed without payment. Thank you again for choosing to insure with Liberty Mutual. If you have any questions or concerns about your claim, please feel free to contact me, either by phone or by email, at your convenience. When contacting me by email, please include your claim number in the subject line.

Sincerely,

Ashley Gliwa
Claims Department

Response from President Service Team

On March 21, 2019, a member from the President Service Team of Liberty Mutual called me to respond to the letter I mailed the President indicating why they would not be covering my claim. The call was followed up by an email. See below:

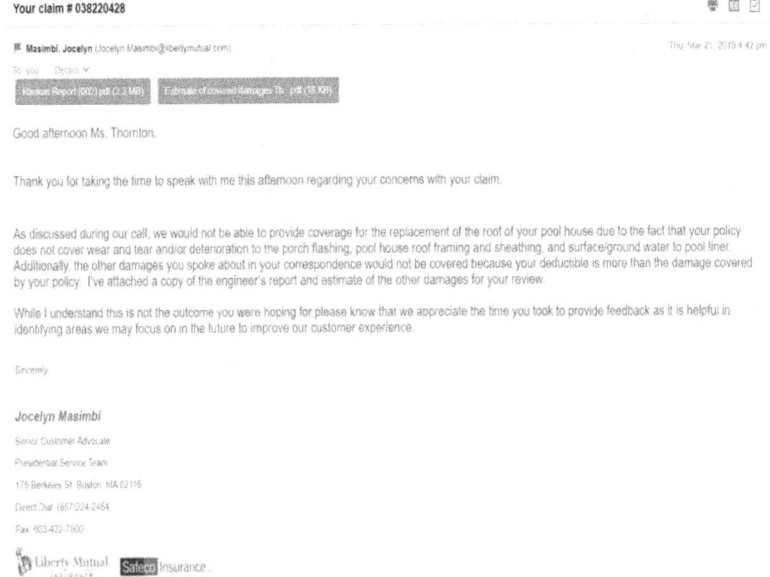

As you can see, the emphasis was put on wear and tear. At the time I obtained the policy Liberty Mutual was aware the home was built in 1989. No one came to my home to check the wear and tear before issuing the policy. Even if the home caves in due to wear and tear, the policy should still cover the structure.

I was maintaining insurance on my home that did not amount to anything. I read my policy closely and according to the policy, the insurance should have covered the damages due to the hurricanes. This company is a FRAUD.

The insurance on my two vehicles with Liberty Mutual was going to be expiring November 25, 2018. So, I let it expire and obtained a policy with GEICO.

Response from NC Dept of Insurance

I received a letter from the NC Department of Insurance dated March 15, 2019, asking if I would like to file a complaint. I subsequently completed a "Request for Assistance" to formally file a complaint against Liberty Mutual Insurance Company. The form and documents were mailed March 25, 2019. As of September 14, 2020, I have not received any additional correspondence from the NC Department of Insurance. See documents below:

NC DEPARTMENT OF INSURANCE
MIKE CAUSEY • COMMISSIONER

CONSUMER SERVICES
Tel 919.807.6750 Fax 919.733.0085

March 15, 2019

Ms. Abbie Thornton
2135 Light Brigade Drive
Matthews, NC 28105

RE: File Number: 2019-03-00643

Dear Ms. Thornton:

The North Carolina Department of Insurance has received a copy of your recent correspondence. Because you have not asked us for information or assistance, we will keep your letter on file without initiating a review, unless we receive further direction from you.

If you would like to file a complaint against your insurance company, please complete the attached request for assistance form. We will forward your completed form to your insurance company and review the company's response for compliance with applicable North Carolina statutes, regulations, and policy requirements.

We can help you understand the circumstances, and we can contact the insurance company on your behalf, but may not provide you with legal opinions or legal representation. If you believe your situation would benefit from direct legal assistance, we recommend that you speak with an independent licensed attorney.

Please do not hesitate to contact me if needed (reference the file number listed above).

Respectfully,

Sheila W., AINS
Property & Casualty Insurance Complaint Analyst
(919) 814-9870

1201 MAIL SERVICE CENTER RALEIGH, NC 27699-1201 WWW.NCDOI.COM

NORTH CAROLINA DEPARTMENT OF INSURANCE
CONSUMER SERVICES DIVISION • 855-408-1212

REQUEST FOR ASSISTANCE

PLEASE PRINT

PERSONAL INFORMATION

YOUR NAME (LAST, FIRST, MI): Thornton, Abbie
☐ Mr. ☒ Ms. ☐ Mrs. ☐ Dr.

ADDRESS: 2135 Light Brigade Drive
CITY: Matthews
STATE: NC
ZIP: 28105

EMAIL ADDRESS: atitacs6@aol.com
MOBILE PHONE: 704-622-6922

RELATIONSHIP TO INSURED: ☒ Self

INSURANCE INFORMATION

NAME OF INSURED: Thornton, Abbie
POLICY OR GROUP NO.: H32-258-132938-70
INSURANCE COMPANY: Liberty Mutual Insurance
CLAIM OR CERTIFICATE NO.: C3 8320428-01
AGENT:
ADJUSTER: Ashley Cluse
DATE OF LOSS: 09/15/2018

TYPE OF INSURANCE: ☒ Homeowners

ARE YOU REPRESENTED BY AN ATTORNEY IN THIS MATTER? ☒ No

ARE YOU COVERED UNDER THE N.C. STATE HEALTH PLAN? ☒ No
ARE YOU COVERED UNDER A SELF-FUNDED EMPLOYER PLAN? ☒ No
ARE YOU REQUESTING ASSISTANCE WITH FILING A MEDICAL APPEAL FOR DENIED MEDICAL SERVICES? ☒ No

DETAILS OF COMPLAINT

See documents in File Number - 2019-03-00643

Since I was in the process of selling my house, I decided to keep the insurance "as is" so I would not have to deal with another insurance company.

I received the following check on my homeowner's policy, not sure why.

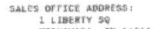

Consent Rate

Not only does Liberty Mutual not provide the coverage that is stated in their homeowner's policy, but they also charge a rate that is much higher than the rate that is suggested by the North Carolina Rate Bureau. They can charge up to 250% of the rate that the NC Rate Bureau recommends. In my policy, the rate was 19% higher than the NC Rate Bureau's rate. Liberty Mutual implies that in the suggested rate, the risk has not been adequately reflected in the NC Rate Bureau's rate. They also require that you sign a document accepting the rate, and if you do not, they will not cover you. This is considered highway robbery and I am appalled that the NC Insurance Commission allows this to happen. See documents below:

Liberty Mutual Insurance
P.O. Box 9009
Dover, NH 03821-9942

P7D09S00100217 - 475563
ABBIE THORNTON
2135 LIGHT BRIGADE DR
MATTHEWS, NC 28105

Policy Number: H3225813243870
PIN: 08877

September 7, 2017

IMMEDIATE ATTENTION - RESPONSE REQUIRED

Dear Abbie,

Your Liberty Mutual Insurance home policy is scheduled to renew on 11/01/2017. As you will see, the premium amount offered by Liberty Mutual on the enclosed "Consent to Rate" form exceeds the North Carolina Rate Bureau (NCRB) standard premium. In order to continue to provide the best insurance protection that we can for our customers, we must charge rates that more accurately reflect the risks associated with home coverage. The NCRB standard premium is not always adequate to cover repair costs in the event of a loss, and writing coverage at the NCRB rate could compromise the service our customers expect.

What does this mean to me?
To keep your home policy, please sign and return the enclosed "Consent to Rate" form in the postage-paid envelope. If you prefer, you may sign the "Consent to Rate" form electronically by visiting our website administered by our trusted partner, Quality Planning ("QPC") at **MyLibertyCTR.PropertyPolicyUpdate.com**. You will need your policy number and PIN, which are listed at the top right side of this page.

We will no longer be able to offer you coverage if the "Consent to Rate" form is not signed and returned to us prior to your renewal effective date 11/01/2017. After receiving your signed and dated consent form, we'll continue to provide home coverage at the rate outlined in your renewal policy package.

If you have any questions, please contact us at 1-704-847-8406 and one of our representatives will be happy to assist you.

Thank you for insuring with Liberty Mutual. We appreciate your business.

Sincerely,

Liberty Mutual Insurance

Liberty Mutual Office
10720 SIKES PLACE, STE 150
CHARLOTTE, NC 28277
704-847-8406/704-845-8359

Policy Number: H3225813243870
Policy Period: 11/01/2017 to 11/01/2018
Effective Date of Proposed Rate: 11/01/2017

ABBIE THORNTON
2135 LIGHT BRIGADE DR
MATTHEWS, NC 28105

Action Required: Sign and Return Form to Continue Coverage for your Property

North Carolina Consent to Rate

"Consent to Rate" property coverage requires your written consent to the rate for your policy when it exceeds the rates proposed by the North Carolina Rate Bureau. Insurers often propose a higher rate for property coverage that more accurately reflects the risk associated with this type of coverage.

What does this mean to you?
To provide your consent to your current rate summarized below, we request that you sign and return this form.

- If you sign and return the form: Liberty Mutual will continue to provide this coverage.

- If you DO NOT sign and return the form: Liberty Mutual CANNOT provide this coverage.

SUMMARY OF COVERAGE AND RATE
Type of Property: Homeowners
Address of Insured Property: Same as mailing address above
Coverage A: $730,700
Deductible: $2,500
Named Storm Deductible:

North Carolina Rate Bureau rate for property coverage: $1,653
Liberty Mutual's rate for property coverage: $1,964
The total percentage increase above the North Carolina Rate Bureau proposed rate is 19%.

This consent to rate applies to property coverage for the address shown above. I understand and consent to Liberty Mutual's rate shown above even though it is in excess of the manual rate established by the North Carolina Rate Bureau. I also understand that the rate does not exceed 250 percent of the manual rate and that coverage for this risk is available through the NC Joint Underwriting Association. I understand that my consent to such coverages, rates, and deductibles shall apply to any renewal, reinstatement, substitute, amended, altered or modified policy with this company.

X _Abbie Thornton_   9/16/2017
Signature of named insured   Date

X _____   _____
Signature of named insured   Date

PROP 013 02 12

Where Are They today (9/16/2020)

Based on the chart below, the renewal and retention rate for Liberty Mutual Auto and Homeowners insurance has steadily decreased over the last six quarters (Q1 2019 - Q2 2020), especially for homeowners' renewals.

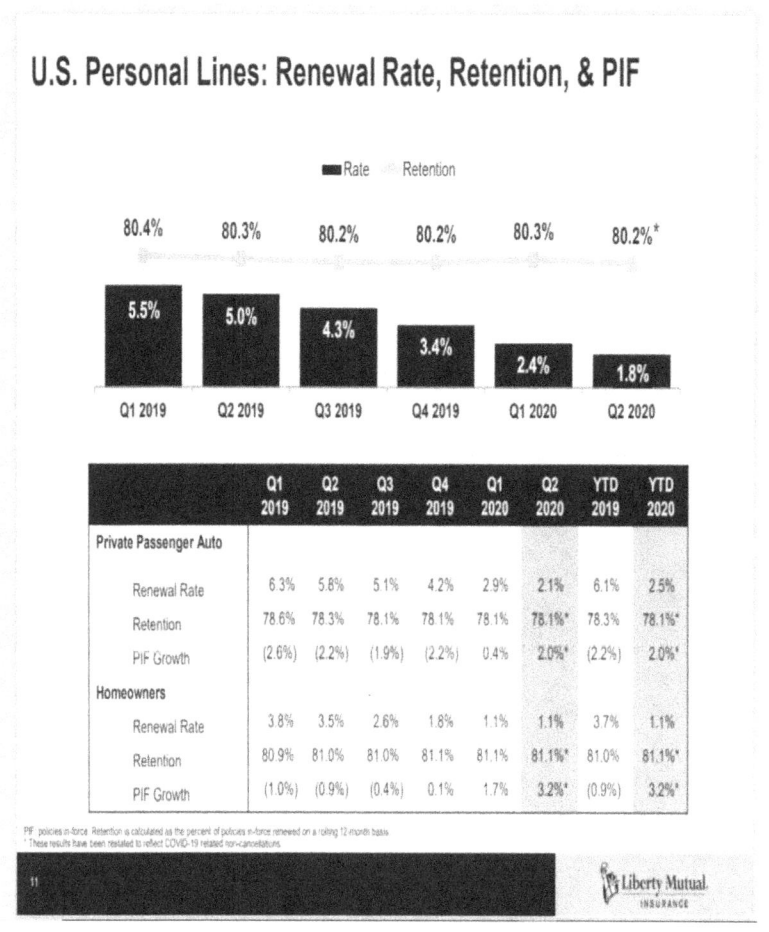

PART VII

MISCELLANEOUS

LETTER 21: Bunion Surgery
(Charlotte Foot Clinic) - December 7, 2007

During the latter part of 2007, I was experiencing some pain with the bunion near my big toe on my left foot. After researching foot doctors, I decided to go to the Charlotte Foot Clinic for surgery.

As I look back, I realize a lot of these medical services providers have found ways to rip the insurance companies off.

Nevertheless, I was told that the insurance company may send checks to me, and if they did, I would need to turn those checks over to the Charlotte Foot Clinic. At the time this sounded reasonable to me. My only concern was that no money would be coming out of my pocket.

So, I scheduled and had the surgery. After a few weeks, I experienced an infection on my left foot. My dry skin was just falling off like a dead person. The doctor had not given me the correct directions on how to properly care for my foot until it healed. Nevertheless, I had a friend that was a Pharmacist that helped me during this period.

During this time, I was traveling to Massachusetts to work. I had to keep my leg elevated during the day and change out and clean my bandages mid-day while at work. Some of my co-workers were very accommodating while helping to ensure my movements were limited during the day. The only time I left my chair was to go to the restroom.

I received an itemized statement from the Foot Clinic dated 11/30/2007 indicating I had an outstanding balance that needed to be paid. These were charges that the insurance company did not reimburse them for because they were considered excess charges. See my response in letter below dated 12/7/2007.

2135 Light Brigade Drive
Matthews, NC 28105
December 7, 2007

Charlotte Foot Clinic
4016 Wilkinson Blvd, Suite A
Charlotte, NC 28208

Subject: Itemized Statement

This memo is in response to the itemized statement dated as of 11/30/2007. It was my understanding from my discussion with you, that after you had received all of the checks that were sent to me in error by Blue Cross Blue Shield (BCBS) that was due to some coding error, my account would be credited for all amounts that were not reimbursed by BCBS.

Amounts that are not reimbursed by BCBS are considered excess charges.

This implies that my account balance should be $0.00 as you have received all the reimbursements from BCBS.

I would appreciate you making the necessary adjustments and send me an updated statement.

Sincerely,

Abbie Thornton

Conclusion: The Charlotte Foot Clinic subsequently sent me a statement indicating I had no outstanding balances.

LETTER 22: Parking Lot Scam
(Habitat Restore) - November 2014

Memo to the File

On Friday, October 31, 2014, I visited the Habitat Restore store on 1133 North Wendover Road, Charlotte, NC.

During my visit, I purchased a desk. My friend came to the store to have the desk loaded on his truck. The desk was loaded at approximately 3:00pm.

After the desk was loaded, I left the store, but my friend stayed a little longer to purchase some other items.

On Saturday morning, November 1, 2014 my friend called me to tell me that a white man approached him while his truck was still in front of the store. The white man asked him if he knew the owner of this "tag number" (TITACS). The white man showed my friend a picture of my tag on his cell phone. My friend indicated he did know the owner of the car to which this tag belonged.

The white man then indicated to my friend that this person had backed into his trailer/vehicle earlier during the week.

My friend said he told the white man that was not possible because I work out of town during the week and had just got back in town from Philadelphia. My friend said the white man walked off after he told him that was not possible.

I went to my garage to check to see if maybe this person had hit my car while in the parking lot at Habitat Restore to try to get money for damages that may have already been done to his vehicle/trailer. There was no damage to my car.

> **Conclusion:** It appears this white man is canvassing parking lots looking for individuals to target for an obvious scam of his. We called the Habitat store to report this to the Manager so this person could be arrested but were unable to get through to anyone on the phone.

I documented this incident in the event the police department contacted me concerning this allegation.

Sincerely,

Abbie Thornton

LETTER 23: Mentors and Protégé
(Warren Buffett) - October 6, 2016

During the process of me writing my book "***From Welfare to a Millionaire***", which was published in 2019; I was thinking about the mentoring giants during my life. I wanted to focus on the areas of education, career, finance, and my life.

Dr. Percy J. Vaughn, Dean of College of Business was my education mentor while I attended Alabama State University from 1977 to 1981. He was also instrumental in me obtaining my first job. Dr. Percy J. Vaughn was my idol while in college at Alabama State University. He was very instrumental in ensuring that his students had the necessary tools to compete in the job market. Additionally, he exposed us to resources and companies to ensure our educational skills were adequately aligned. He was deceased in 2018.

Alana Robinson, CIO was my career mentor while working at Sara Lee Hosiery in 1996 and has continued to mentor me over the years. Alana Robinson took me under her wings while she was the CIO at Sara Lee Hosiery. As I mentioned in my book, I attended several professional events and conferences with her, such as the Black MBA Conference, Jock and Jill, and the Top Black Leadership Conference where they had the top black individuals in the Information Technology field in attendance. I was provided an opportunity to listen to great minds and see how successful and fulfilling I could become.

My Lord and Savior is my mentor for my purpose driven life. My Lord and Savior is the light of my life. He is my wheel in the middle of the wheel. He is the first and the last, Alpha and Omega, the beginning, and the end. He is my provider, he is my rock, he is my strength, he is my sustainer, and he is my salvation. He is Love. He is my all and all. He is the great "I AM".

Letter to Warren Buffett

When I started to think about my financial mentor, I realized I did not have one. So, I decided to write Warren Buffett and ask if he would be my mentor in my finances. Below is the following letter I mailed to Mr. Warren Buffett:

2135 Light Brigade Drive
Matthews, North Carolina 28105
October 6, 2016

Warren E. Buffett, CEO
Berkshire Hathaway, Inc.
3555 Farnam Street, Suite 1440
Omaha, Nebraska 68131

Dear Mr. Buffett:

I know you are an extremely busy man. I am writing you to request that you become my mentor. I would appreciate ten (10) minutes of your time each month to mentor me on accomplishing my goals, as well as sharing your wisdom with me.

I am a single mother of two from North Carolina, and my goal is to become a billionaire. I have several product ideas, and I am in the process of writing my first book.

My phone number is 704-622-6982, and email address is atitacs@aol.com; however, I understand that you don't send emails.

I would appreciate your consideration.

Sincerely,

Response for Buffett Assistant
■■

On November 3, 2016, I received the following email response from Carrie Sova, Warren Buffett's assistant:

> Dear Abbie:
>
> Until recently, Mr. Buffett has tried to respond personally, even if briefly, to most unsolicited letters and emails. However, the quantity of mail coming to him has exploded – requests for investment or career advice, employment applications, internship, invitations, book endorsements, autographs, photographs, financial assistance, etc. Some of the letter writers even ask for golf games or letters of recommendation. Many have a favored cause in which they wish him to become interested. Most of these letters would require him to spend 15-30 minutes of his time if he were to formulate and dictate a thoughtful response.
>
> I hope you understand the necessity for this form.
>
> Carrie Sova
> Berkshire Hathaway

■■

I responded back as follows on November 3, 2016:

> Hello Carrie:
>
> How are you? I appreciate you taking the time to acknowledge receipt of my letter. I truly understand that Mr. Buffett is an extremely busy man.

I believe we have not because we ask not. I also believe our paths will cross.

Abbie,

■■

Follow-up Letter to Warren Buffett
Since Mr. Buffett did not specifically say "NO", I decided to send a follow-up letter. Below is the follow-up letter I mailed April 2017:

2135 Light Brigade Drive
Matthews, North Carolina 28105
April 18, 2017

Warren E. Buffett, CEO
Berkshire Hathaway, Inc.
3555 Farnam Street, Suite 1440
Omaha, Nebraska 68131

Dear Mr. Buffett:

This letter is a follow-up to a letter I sent you that was dated October 6, 2016. Within that letter, I asked if you would consider becoming my mentor to provide some guidance in helping me to accomplish some of my goals. Five minutes of your time on a quarterly basis would have a significant impact on my life.

Your assistant, Carrie Sova indicated that you get all types of requests for your time and resources, and that your incoming mail has exploded and it is difficult to keep up. I truly understand.

I may be viewed as just a single mother from North Carolina, however, I believe I will have a significant impact on the world one day. I just need someone of your caliber to steer me in the right direction.

My phone number is 704-622-6982, and email address is atitacs@aol.com.

Sincerely,

Abbie Thornton

As of the writing of this book, I have not received another response from Mr. Warren Buffett.

LETTER 24: Racoons in the Ceiling
(The Tradition Apartments) - June 2020

I lived on the first floor of the apartment complex. There were two separate families overhead on the second floor. I was always hearing various noises from the family above and did not think much of a noise when I heard it.

During the March – April 2020 time frame, the Apartment buildings were being painted. Also, this was the time that Covid-19 hit, and school and businesses were being closed. The city was pretty much shut down.

During Covid-19 shutdown, I was spending more quiet time at home and was staying up later than normal. I started to hear this "scratching" noise that sounded like a rat. I started to pay close attention to the noise to pinpoint where I was hearing it when I heard it. The noise was usually near the front entrance and the kitchen.

I noticed that when the painters were painting my apartment building, some of the "Soffit" under the overhang had come apart and was on the ground. I thought the painter would replace it after they finished the painting. Those pieces of materials were on the ground for months.

One day I was coming home, and a couple stopped me as I was pulling into the driveway and said that they just saw a raccoon crawl into the hole that had been exposed because of pieces of the roof overhang coming apart while the contractors were painting the building. I immediately reported this to the Apartment Management.

A few days later, I saw this huge raccoon walking across the apartment parking lot coming from the building I lived in. The apartment management came and closed the hole up with a piece of wood. I noticed there was a smaller hole at the other end of the roof, and I inquired about them closing that hole up also. The maintenance person indicated that hole was too small for the racoon to enter. The next day I noticed that hole had gotten larger and another piece of the "Soffit" had been removed.

I then started to pay close attention to the noises I was hearing. One night I woke up and there was "squealing" overhead in the ceiling. It got to the point where I could not sleep at night or feel at peace in my apartment anymore.

In the meantime, the apartment management put a cage out to try and catch the raccoon. I saw the raccoon looking at the bait in the cage and it just keep going. The next day the bait was gone and there was no raccoon in the cage.

A few weeks went by and the raccoon had not been caught. The apartment management then contracted with "Critter Control" to try to catch the racoon. Critter Control put a cage on top of the roof near the entrance/exit of the raccoon. The next day the raccoon was caught. I informed the apartment management that the raccoon had been caught and they needed to contact "Critter Control" to come get it.

In the meantime, the temperature was very hot, and the raccoon was in the cage on top of the roof. The Critter Control company did not come and get the racoon that day, or the next. So, some friendly animal activist knocked the cage off the roof and released the raccoon. The raccoon returned to the roof because we found out it had at least two babies still overhead in the ceiling.

By this time, I am furious and afraid to go into my apartment. The noises got louder, and it seemed as if the raccoons were trying to escape through my furnace area. I had to put a nightstand and chair at the furnace door to keep them from coming into my apartment.

I decided I could no longer sleep in the apartment and requested a temporary apartment to sleep in until they removed the raccoons. I was given a one-bedroom apartment to sleep in with my air mattress. After a week, the racoon still had not been removed. I wrote the following letter requesting to be moved to a new apartment permanently altogether. See below:

10555 Parkhouse Lane
Charlotte, NC 28269
June 15, 2020

Mr. Michael Atkins, Property Manager
The Tradition at Mallard Creek
2525 Crescent View Drive
Charlotte, NC 28269

Subject: Raccoons in Apartment 10555 Parkhouse Lane

As you are aware, on Friday June 12, 2020 the **Animal Control Company** came and set two traps to try and catch the raccoons that have been over my apartment ceiling for at least the last three (3) weeks. A trap was put on the roof and one was put on the ground between 12:30 pm and 1:00 pm.

At approximately 4:00pm, the trap had caught one of the larger raccoons. One of your maintenance employees took a picture of the raccoon in the trap and sent it to you. It was indicated that you called the **Animal Control Company** concerning the trap catching the raccoon and they would be coming Saturday morning, June 13, 2020 to get the raccoon.

At 1:00pm on Saturday, June 13, 2020. The raccoon was still in the trap on top of the roof. At approximately 4:00pm on Saturday, I noticed that the cage had been removed from the roof and was on the ground, and the raccoon was not it.

It is my understanding that several tenants had called the office on Saturday complaining about the raccoon being in that trap for almost 24 hours without it being removed; and they knocked that cage down from the roof and released the raccoon. *(I would imagine these were animal activists.)* As of Sunday, no one from the **Animal Control Company** still has not come back to the apartment.

I was fearful that the raccoon returned the apartment to be with its babies. So, on Sunday, I asked a male friend to go the apartment with me so I could take a shower. Based on the noise we heard around the "Furnace", it sounded as if the racoons were recking havoc. My friend put two night stands up against the door where the furnace is in the event the racoons tore through the duct work, so that they would not get in my apartment.

On Thursday, June 11, 2020 I had called the maintenance team indicating I had heard that noise around the furnace. When they got there, they assumed it was coming from the furnace as the condensation was draining. I made it clear then, that was not what I was hearing.

At this point, I am afraid to go into the apartment alone. I work from home and I need access to my computer, files, and internet service. I also have my grandson during the day, and I am fearful of potential "rabies" or other viruses spreading through the vents, etc.

I am requesting to move out of this apartment (10555 Parkhouse Lane) into another three-bedroom apartment, with a garage on the bottom level as soon as possible. I am afraid to live in that apartment.

Please let me know when I can start the move so that I can make the necessary arrangements. I appreciate your attention.

Sincerely,

Abbie Thornton

I started moving out of this apartment on June 16, 2020. A few weeks later, I noticed someone had moved into 10555 Parkhouse Lane. The hole where the racoons were entering, and exiting was still open. I went by the apartment again in August 2020, and the hole was still open.

GETTING OFF THE GRID

Over the last 40 years and during most of my adult life, I have been very conscientious about handling my business. My bills were paid on time; taxes paid when due; I followed through on all correspondences; I returned phone calls within 24 hours; and I responded to emails and texts on a timely basis.

It seemed as if each day was a "TEST". There was always some issue I had to resolve because of someone else not doing their job properly or following through on their end. Almost every encounter with an organization or even individuals resulted in incompleteness, confusion, misinformation, etc. For example:

   a. I had a tree cut down in my yard. A friend recommended a gentleman to grind the tree stump out. The tree stump was inside of my 'red rock' bed at the front of the house. As the gentleman was grinding out the tree stump, saw dust was covering my 'red rocks'. So, I had to blow out the saw dust where possible, and then I had to buy some additional rocks to cover the ones that were covered with the saw dust I was unable to blow away from the rocks. This cost me more money and my time.
   b. An Air Conditioning Technician came to my house to blow out my drainage pipe from the air conditioning unit in the attic. He did not have the part to cover one of the pipes. A friend of mine volunteered to go to Lowe's to get the covering for the pipe. When he

put the covering over the pipe, he did not secure it. I questioned him about not securing it and he said it did not matter if he secured it or not. A few days later I noticed a wet spot in my ceiling which was a result of him not securing the covering on the pipe. As a result, I had to paint my ceiling and wall below the attic.

c. I had a leak in my toilet. One of my neighbors across the street professes to be a plumber. He came to my home to repair the leak. I paid him the requested fee. I put a bucket below the area where the leak was to ensure it no longer leaked. When I came back in a few hours, there was water in the bucket. I then called a certified plumber. I did not mention to the neighbor that the toilet was still leaking because I did not want anymore "on the job" training in my house.

I was in my last home for approximately 16 years. My average property tax bill was approximately $4,000 annually during this period. This means that I have paid $64,000 in property taxes to the government. Even if a person pays off their mortgage, they still must pay property taxes to the government.

The $64,000 could have gone towards me reducing my mortgage loan amount for those 16 years. What is the purpose of owning a home, and you must pay to live in it for the remainder of your life? If you do not pay the property taxes, the government will take your home away from you.

The letters I have written are examples of some of the encounters and hurdles I had to address and resolve. I have spent so much time and energy. I sometime think how I could have used this energy and time to contribute to making this a better world to live in and find my life's destiny.

THE END

www.ingramcontent.com/pod-product-compliance
Lightning Source LLC
Chambersburg PA
CBHW060830220526
45466CB00003B/1051